yellow highlight 5/15/97

371.1   Pronin, Barbara
Pro   Substitute teaching; a handbook for
c.3   hassle-free subbing.   St. Martin's, c1983.
            241 p.

            1. Substitute teachers - Handbooks, manuals,
            etc. I. Title
13.95   LC 82-16865

SUBSTITUTE TEACHING

SUBSTITUTE TEACHING

A Handbook for Hassle-Free Subbing

by BARBARA PRONIN

ST. MARTIN'S PRESS NEW YORK

Design by Mina Greenstein

Library of Congress Cataloging in Publication Data

Pronin, Barbara.
  Substitute teaching.

  Includes index.
  1. Substitute teachers—Handbooks, manuals, etc.
I. Title.
LB2844.1.S8P76   1983   371.1'4122   82–16865
ISBN 0-312-77481-8

FIRST EDITION
10 9 8 7 6 5 4 3 2 1

FOR MY MOTHER,
> who believes I can do anything . . .

MY HUSBAND,
> who encourages this outrageousness . . .

AND MY CHILDREN,
> whose outrageousness is encouraging.

For their assistance and kind support on the road to this book, my heartfelt thanks to: Judy Tudhope, Ceil Forman, Janie Wiles, Georgia Florentine and her staff at Ben Lomond School, Florence Feiler, Karen Johnsen, John P. LaRue of the Los Angeles County Superintendent's office, Chuck Kaufman and the Los Angeles County Public Library System—Children's Division, Leanna Landsmann and Instructor *magazine, Dick Lochte of* The Los Angeles Times *. . . and hundreds of individuals and school districts who responded with such heartening enthusiasm.*

BARBARA PRONIN

CONTENTS

INTRODUCTION

As long as there are children in school and teachers with sick leave, there will always be a need for good substitutes: those trusty pinch-hitting teachers who can step to the plate at a moment's notice.

Where do these subs come from? Some are former teachers who no longer wish to work full-time. Others are recent college graduates who, in this age of shrinking student enrollment, are unable to find full-time positions.

But many, like me—possibly like you—are mothers and fathers, artists and writers, curious, busy, interested people who have never taught before.

Surprised? So was I, when I learned I was eligible to substitute teach in California.

I had been casting about for something to do in my spare time now that my children were in school. I had a bachelor's degree, and my background included professional acting, probation work, and some writing from time to time. None of those areas now seemed just right for one reason or another.

I wanted to be home when my children were, but, after years of diapers and baby talk for company, I wanted to get out and meet people. Yet, interesting jobs were tough to find on a part-time basis and I didn't want to work full-time.

One day I had a visit from a friend up the coast whose background was similar to mine. When I learned she was subbing, my eyes opened wide. "How on earth did you get into teaching?"

"I called the school district one day," she said, "and found out that with my B.A. I could substitute."

"Hmmm," I mused. Perhaps that was true in the small town in which she lived. But here, in Los Angeles County? Still, my curiosity got the best of me at last, and I telephoned my local school district.

I've been subbing ever since.

Most subs, I have since learned, want a part-time career with flexible hours and decent pay. They want to supplement their income doing interesting work in a professional setting. Some are college graduates. Many are not. Most never majored in education.

They qualify as substitute teachers on the basis of their educational or professional work experience, and they enter our children's academic world with a fresh outlook, eager dedication—and little or no formal training.

Some of them do wonderfully well. They meet the challenge with skill and imagination and are soon working as many days per month as they wish.

Others, just as qualified and just as well intentioned, have difficulty coping with the needs and demands of thirty children at once. They need help understanding group dynamics, classroom practices, dealing with new situations every day. They become harried, frustrated, disappointed —often dropping out of the field, which needs new people all the time. Where did I go wrong? they wonder. Is subbing really for me?

Substitute teaching can provide a rewarding, well-paid, part-time career for many who never dreamed they could do it. But many questions must be answered, of course.

And that's what this book is all about.

Whether you're an old hand at subbing or brand new in the field, even—especially!—if you're only beginning to contemplate the prospect of subbing at all, there is something for you in the coming chapters.

How can I qualify in my state? How much can I earn? What do I do?

What's going on in classrooms today? Do I have to be a fountain of knowledge?

What about preparation? Procedures? How do I handle discipline? And what do I do when the lesson is over and there's still half an hour to fill?

Just what am I getting into, here? Will I like it? Will the students like me?

In the following pages, I'll try to give you an objective look at education today, a preview of what to expect in the classroom and how to handle new situations before the need arises.

You'll find hundreds of creative new ideas and impromptu activities to round out your day with a minimum of fuss—the kinds of activities children like.

Here is subbing with its joys and all its complexities— and here's how to make it hassle-free.

Welcome to the world of subbing. I love it. Maybe you will, too!

PART ONE

The ABCs of Subbing

Starting a career in substitute teaching is a little like going on a blind date. You open the door, hope for the best, and if it doesn't work out—you get a headache.

The reason for this sad state of affairs is that many subs don't have the foggiest idea what they're getting into. In Part One, we will explore the whos, hows, and whys of subbing. Who can do it? How? And why bother?

The more you know before you get started, the more successful that blind date can be. So grab your coat and open that door. Have I got a career for you!

1.

What Does a Sub Do?

Let me go on record as saying here and now that substitute teaching is fun. It is necessary to like children, of course, and to be open-minded and flexible enough to face new classes daily. But if you are a reasonably friendly, outgoing person with a general knowledge of the basic subject areas, you have the attributes.

As you might expect from the term "substitute teacher," the sub is a stand-in for the regular teacher in any given classroom on any given day.

Whether the regular teacher is out sick, attending a conference, or stuck in a snowstorm on the slopes of Aspen, every school district must have at hand a roster of people—familiarly dubbed as "subs"—who can, at very short notice, step into the classroom and take over the duties of the teacher.

It comes as no news to most of us that the American population is shrinking. The high cost of living and our concern for the welfare of future generations is resulting in smaller families. Schools are closing here and there because of lower student enrollment, and newly certified teachers sometimes have difficulty finding jobs.

Yet, in a recent questionnaire sent at random to more than a hundred school districts nationwide, one hundred percent responded overwhelmingly that they have an ongoing need for substitutes! Someone must stand at the head of each class when the regular teacher is out.

But what does the sub do?

Since the primary obligation of every teacher is to teach, you are correct in assuming that you, as a sub, will be expected to instruct students in all of the basic subject areas from first grade penmanship to high school algebra depending upon the grade level of the teacher you are replacing.

Does this mean that you must be a whiz in every subject? That the intricacies of trigonometry must be as easy for you as simple addition? Of course not. What it does mean is that you should be aware of the *kinds* of subject matter taught at the various grade levels and have a passing acquaintance with them.

You must also be aware of the differences in attitude and behavior at various grade levels so that you can determine which age groups you will be most comfortable with as a sub.

In a later chapter we will discuss these academic and behavioral differences in detail so that you can make an intelligent decision about where you would most like to be. For now, suffice it to say that, yes, you will be expected to teach.

You will be expected, too, to maintain control of the class. While quiet times are still necessary and desirable—as during the taking of tests, for example, or when all students are working on a simultaneous assignment—the days of silent classrooms many of us remember from our youths have more or less gone the way of white buck shoes and poodle skirts.

Today's classrooms, as we shall see, are often active and multilevel. That is, more than one grade level may be represented in a room or the children may be grouped according to their skill. While this is efficient in terms of learning, it can also mean that you must have eyes in the back of your head (remember the way your mother did?).

When you are not accustomed to dealing with thirty children at once it takes a keen eye and a cool head to develop firm organization. You need to know what's going on in all corners of the classroom for the day to progress in a smooth and orderly fashion.

As one sub recently told me, "The first time I worked with a special reading group I told the rest of the class to read silently to themselves and I assumed they would do just that. By the time I looked up to call the second group forward, there was bedlam—and I hadn't even realized!"

Before long, you will discover that the surest way to keep "bedlam" from your door is to keep students busy and happily occupied, especially when you need to work with individual groups. Timefillers (Chapter 12) and a little common sense will help.

You must become familiar with standard school procedures such as fire drills, playground rules, and the like, for you will be expected to supervise and enforce them. A later chapter will steer you toward learning these basic procedures before you enter the classroom. When the appropriate bell sounds, *you* should instruct the children about its meaning, not the other way around.

You will perform whatever extra duties the regular teacher was scheduled to perform on a given day. The task of supervising children during recesses and lunch hour, and in the lunchroom itself, is often divided among staff members who may give up a portion of their own free time on a rotating basis in order to do it. While it may seem that teachers are absent only on rainy days when they have bus duty, rest assured this minor inconvenience comes with the territory.

If the teacher was scheduled to attend a staff meeting you may be required to attend in his or her place, taking adequate notes.

In kindergarten through sixth grade classrooms (K–6),

particularly where students are in the same room all day, you may find yourself with blocks of unscheduled time, which you will be expected to fill with choices of your own.

Every absentee teacher leaves a lesson plan of some sort for the substitute's use. This may be in the form of a note to you or on a schedule listed in the plan book. Needless to say, some lesson plans are far more complete and detailed than others.

At those times when the daily lesson plan is skimpy or is altered for some reason—for example, band practice is canceled or a scheduled film does not arrive—you may have free time on your hands. Subs are encouraged to use this time to introduce their own projects and activities.

Part Three of this book is filled with hundreds of indoor and outdoor ideas to help you use free time happily and creatively and to get you started using your own special talents and skills to fill your bag of tricks.

Last but not least you will be expected to behave in an ethical and professional manner. You will arrive on time and stay until your tasks are complete. You will dress in a manner befitting a teacher, uphold the district rules for health and safety, and use school property and materials with care.

You will treat each school, each class, each day's assignment with equal enthusiasm and aplomb. You may have your favorites, for every school has a "personality" all its own, but you will make it a point never to openly compare one school or staff with another. You can't win friends or influence people by literally carrying tales out of school. If you are quick to criticize School A, muses the staff, what must you be saying about us?

Subbing assures such built-in variety that you will never be bored. That's what makes it such fun. With rare exceptions, your days will be exciting and rewarding both for you and for your students.

Of course there may be days when you would rather be penned in a barnyard full of chattering chickens. You may thank a higher power that certain children do not live under your roof, and there may be times when you wonder why you didn't choose trucking over college. Relax. Every teacher has these moments.

But *you* have the option of picking and choosing when and where you will teach. This is a part-time career, after all, and you'll work only as much as you wish. If Mrs. Glutz's fifth grade has all the earmarks of a madhouse, take comfort from the fact that you need never return there again. (And pity poor Mrs. Glutz.)

You have the freedom to use whatever lesson plans have been offered by the regular teacher and to supplement them with whatever enriching experiences you bring to the classroom to make for a more pleasant day.

And you have the luxury of meeting new people daily and of sharing in the joy of a child's new discoveries, emerging personality, and youthful energy without the day to day responsibility of channeling that energy into routine academic expectations.

In short, you get to do the fun things for which many regular teachers simply do not have the time. You can approach each day with a sense of adventure and spontaneity.

What you will not have to do is prepare long-term lesson plans, assign grades to report cards, confer with parents, or get involved with the mountain of paperwork and meetings with which most teachers have to contend.

Best of all, when you leave the classroom at the end of the day you will not be burdened with stacks of papers to correct, next month's Open House to plan, or the senior play to direct. You can leave the school grounds with a clear conscience and use the rest of the day for your personal and particular pursuits. For those of you with family responsibilities, artistic or educational commitments, or a proclivity toward afternoon naps, this advantage is not inconsiderable. Subs have the added bonus of little or no homework!

Lest we seem to imply that substitute teachers have the

best of all possible lots, it seems fair to point out that there are some equalizing factors.

For one thing, subs are not paid anything resembling the daily equivalent of a regular teacher's paycheck. Teachers are not highly paid to begin with and, for the privilege of escaping the long-term responsibility of the teacher, you will be paid at a lower daily rate.

For another, in most cases you will not be eligible for the package of benefits including insurance, pensions, and the like to which regular teachers are entitled. While this is typical for part-time employment in most fields, it is a point you may wish to consider.

It should be noted that if you are interested in (and qualified for) long-term subbing assignments in which you are replacing the regular teacher for an extended period of time, your rate of pay and attendant benefits will increase in direct proportion to the long-term duties that you take on. More about pay scales and benefits will be found in Chapter 3.

Third, for all the inherent fun and spontaneity, the sub's task is not child's play. You are expected to maintain order and an atmosphere of learning in a situation that differs greatly from that of the regular teacher.

You may be familiar with the basic subject matter, but you cannot draw from a background of continuity or familiarity with your students' level of skill.

Furthermore, as a sub, you have no regular place in the pecking order of the school faculty. The extent of your authority is therefore questionable, at least in the minds of some students. This can make discipline a little tricky.

Most important of all, you lack the single greatest piece of leverage available to every regular teacher: *the power of the grade*.

With experience, and by mastering the techniques suggested here, you will gain a measure of confidence and authority. Your face will become recognized on various campuses and your reputation for fairness, fun, and knowledge will precede you. That helps. But experience and reputation notwithstanding, the power of the grade will elude you. And it is grades—those little letters A, B, C, D, and F—for which many students perform their best (or worst!) work.

An A from the teacher buys for the student parental approval and sometimes extra privileges. An F can send the world crashing about his feet. It is the regular teacher who, by and large, dispenses these harbingers of fortune. Students are aware that your presence in the classroom for a day or two will not measurably affect their grades. This knowledge can act as an open invitation to goof off, misbehave, and generally try your patience without too much fear of reprisal.

It is essential, therefore, that you as a sub develop concrete ways to offer evidence that your own assessment of their work *does* count.

As you become familiar with the ideas in this book you will learn about positive reinforcement and assertive discipline. You will master the tools for making your part-time teaching career truly hassle-free. It is through the use of such things as "superstars," "sour apples," and "brain-teaser champs" (see Chapter 10) that you may gain your greatest measure of control. Certainly you will have a start in developing your own methods for maintaining the happy and productive classrooms for which every sub must strive.

There are rumors afoot that substitute teaching is a matter of survival at best. Proponents of this view would have us believe that subs must necessarily be subjected to chaos and lack of cooperation; that any learning that takes place in their classroom is purely coincidental. They regard subs as little more than glorified babysitters who lack initiative and authority.

On the contrary, substitute teachers who enter the field with a clear knowledge of what to expect and who are prepared, confident, and willing to give of themselves perform a vital service and can give an added fillip to our educational system.

Not only will you provide leadership and continuity but you will do it with your own special flair. You will, of course, move within the framework of the regular teacher's long-term goals. But by adding your insights, your talents, *yourself,* you are sharing something no one else can give.

As a sub, you must stand in for the regular teacher and take on the responsibility of moving academic learning forward. You must use whatever materials are at hand and supplement them with innovative, educational, and diverting activities of your own. You must do it in a setting that is casual but correct, friendly but authoritative, and often entirely new to you.

What does a sub do? A sub teaches. And improvises. And enriches. And has a heck of a good time doing it!

2.

Can I Qualify?

Let's begin by saying that it is possible to substitute teach in most of these United States without having regular teacher certification.

Regular certification means a currently valid teaching credential issued by the state in which you live. It is a document held by every regular teacher in the state certifying that he or she has met certain requirements including graduation from an accredited college or university with the appropriate courses in Teacher Education and endorsement in special subject areas.

Usually, teachers have had to spend a specified number of hours in student teaching assignments and may have been required to pass licensing or proficiency examinations.

In other words, preparation for a full-time career in teaching involves the same sort of rigid training necessary for a career in any professional field. This, of course, is as it should be. The long-term education of our children is too important an undertaking to be left in the hands of unqualified or semiprofessional people.

Men and women who substitute in *long-term* positions, when the teacher is absent for a period of weeks or months, are required in most states to fulfill all or most of the qualifications necessary for full-time teaching. These people must be responsible for long-term lesson planning and grading just as the regular teacher would be.

The criteria for long-term subbing vary from state to state both in terms of credential requirements and in the number of consecutive teaching days considered to be "long term." Yet, whatever the criteria in an individual state might be, most administrators agree that regularly certified teachers are preferable for these positions.

But when a teacher is absent for a day or two and when short-term lesson plans can be initiated so that the process of education is uninterrupted, most states and school districts find it necessary and valuable to use qualified semi-professionals as substitute teachers.

These short-term, or day to day, subs must hold a credential as well. But the qualifications for obtaining such credentials are often less stringent and far from standardized.

As in licensing procedures in many other fields, the requirements for substitute teaching credentials are left to the discretion of each state. They are based on current needs and individual preferences and are issued by the state's Department for Teacher Certification. Often, they are applied for with a recommendation by the school district in which you expect to sub.

In order to discover the minimum requirements for substitute credentials in all parts of the country I polled each of the fifty states. More than a hundred randomly chosen school districts were contacted in major cities, suburban areas, and outlying regions. The results are nothing less than staggering.

Every district responding indicated an ongoing need for substitutes. Salary levels differ dramatically. But the dif-

ferences in credential requirements as set forth by every
state are even more dramatic.

A chart at the end of this chapter lists the minimum educational requirements currently acceptable in each state. A
quick survey will reveal that, depending upon where in the
country you live, you may be qualified to substitute teach
with anything ranging from a high school diploma to regular teacher certification!

Sometimes even within a state the requirements are not
standardized but vary with the needs in different areas. Major cities, for example, have more potential subs from
which to draw. Their requirements are somewhat stricter.
In rural areas, where teachers are in shorter supply, the
standards for subs may be relaxed.

Alabama is a case in point. In some areas of the state
high school graduates are acceptable. In others, a minimum
of two years' college is required in addition to workshops
offered by the county in which you will sub.

Generally speaking, if you have or are eligible for regular
teacher certification you can substitute anywhere in either
long- or short-term situations. Even if your certification has
expired or was issued by another state, you may qualify for
a substitute credential in the state in which you now live.
Even states that prefer regular certification are often willing
to waive certain qualifications.

In fact, to the best of my knowledge, there is not a single
state in the union that requires regular teacher certification
in *all* areas of the state or in *all* circumstances for day to
day subs.

In Idaho, regular certificates are necessary in the major
cities, but people with high school diplomas or bachelor's
degrees may sub in the rural areas.

In West Virginia, where a regular certificate is preferred,
some counties offer special training that can qualify people
with bachelor's degrees to substitute within those counties.

In Iowa, Oregon, and Washington regular certification is

also preferred. But certain standards for eligibility such as recency of experience or out-of-state licensing may be waived.

This random sampling could not possibly include every school district in the state. It cannot reflect the fluctuating need for subs in all areas. If you live in a state which, according to the chart, requires regular certification, I urge you to check with several local districts to learn whether you may be eligible to sub under certain conditions or in certain areas. If you live near a state line, check the residency requirements as well. It may be possible for you to sub in the neighboring state.

The fact is it is difficult to find enough regularly certified teachers to meet the constant demand for subs. Furthermore, most educators agree that full training is not necessary to handle day to day substitute teaching.

For this reason—and here comes the good news—most states will issue a provisional substitute credential upon the recommendation of a school district. The term for it may vary. It may be called a "limited," "substandard," or "emergency" credential. In all cases it is issued at the district's request to people who meet specified standards and whom the district wishes to hire.

These standards may include educational background, work experience, and/or experience in working with groups. A desire to teach, an understanding of the job, and a positive outlook may be taken into consideration as well.

Your provisional credential may limit the number of days per year you can work or the areas in which it is valid. It may or may not qualify you for additional employee benefits such as retirement plans or insurance. But if substitute teaching is what you want to do, it will allow you to do just that.

How can you qualify?

In approximately one-third of our states a bachelor's degree (B.A.) will qualify you for a provisional sub's credential, regardless of your major area of study, if you wish to teach at the elementary level. For the high school level you may need to have completed a certain number of courses in the area you wish to teach. This is sometimes called endorsement. You need not have taken education courses or had prior teaching experience, although that would be a desirable bonus.

More than 3,000 such provisional credentials were issued in Los Angeles County alone during the school year 1980–81! Does that give you some idea of how badly subs are needed?

Another one-third of our states will issue substitute credentials to people with sixty to ninety semester hours of college to their credit, provided they have maintained at least a C average. Again, major study area is not of prime importance at the elementary level nor is prior teaching experience.

This allows college students to "earn while they learn" and provides subbing opportunities to countless others as well.

Some 2,000, or nearly one-half, of all the substitutes teaching in the small state of Delaware are subbing with a provisional credential.

In still other states a high school diploma is all that is necessary to qualify for a substitute credential if you can convince the school district that your background, interests, and experience have equipped you to handle the job.

More than one-half of the substitutes teaching in Montgomery County, Alabama, are teaching with these minimal qualifications.

You will need to supply diplomas, transcripts, or other documentation to verify your educational standing. You must comply with state health regulations, which may include having current tuberculosis screening or other procedures. You will pay a fee for processing of your credential by the state. But that, dear friends, is that!

In composing the following chart, I have listed the most current minimal requirements as set forth by each state. Remember that these are minimal requirements and may not apply to every area or situation. Laws do change and needs do vary. In places where the demand for subs exceeds the supply, exceptions are sometimes made.

If you are interested in subbing and can come anywhere close to fulfilling the minimum requirements for your state, do not hesitate to inquire at your local school district office. You may be surprised to learn that you can indeed qualify or that a course or two at a nearby college will make the necessary difference.

Good luck!

Chart I: CAN I QUALIFY?

State	Minimum Requirements	Long-term Requirements
ALABAMA	Law requires high school graduate. Some areas require two years college plus workshops.	Regular Alabama teaching certificate
ALASKA	Bachelor's degree	Regular Alaska teaching certificate
ARIZONA	Bachelor's degree	Regular Arizona teaching certificate
ARKANSAS	High school graduation	Regular Arkansas teaching certificate
CALIFORNIA	Bachelor's degree or 90 semester hours	Regular California teaching certificate
COLORADO	Bachelor's degree or noncurrent certification	Satisfactory performance in short-term assignments
CONNECTICUT	Bachelor's degree	Bachelor's degree

Chart I: CAN I QUALIFY? *(continued)*

State	Minimum Requirements	Long-term Requirements
DISTRICT OF COLUMBIA	60 semester hours college—minimum C average	Regular D.C. teaching certificate
DELAWARE	Some college	Same plus recommendation from district
FLORIDA	Some college	Regular Florida teaching certificate
GEORGIA	High school graduation	Regular Georgia teaching certificate
HAWAII	High school graduation	Regular Hawaii teaching certificate
IDAHO	High school graduation to regular certification depending on area	Regular Idaho teaching certificate
ILLINOIS	Bachelor's degree	B.A. up to 90 days; regular certification thereafter
INDIANA	60 semester hours college	Regular Indiana teaching certificate

State		
Iowa	Must once have held Iowa or non-Iowa certification	Regular Iowa teaching certificate after 90 days
Kansas	60 semester hours college	Regular Kansas teaching certificate after 90 days
Kentucky	64 semester hours college	64 semester hours college plus satisfactory performance
Louisiana	Bachelor's degree	Regular Louisiana teaching certificate
Maine	60 semester hours college	Regular Maine teaching certificate after 60 days
Maryland	60 semester hours college	Regular Maryland teaching certificate
Massachusetts	Bachelor's degree	Regular Massachusetts teaching certificate
Michigan	60 semester hours college	Regular Michigan teaching certificate or work experience

Chart I: CAN I QUALIFY? *(continued)*

State	Minimum Requirements	Long-term Requirements
MINNESOTA	Bachelor's degree	Regular Minnesota teaching certificate
MISSISSIPPI	60 semester hours college	Regular Mississippi teaching certificate
MISSOURI	60 semester hours college; B.A. for more than 90 teaching days per year	Regular Missouri teaching certificate after 90 days
MONTANA	Just short of bachelor's degree	Regular Montana teaching certificate after 30 days
NEBRASKA	Expired regular certification	Regular Nebraska teaching certificate
NEVADA	62 semester hours college	62 semester hours college
NEW HAMPSHIRE	Bachelor's degree plus some education credits	B.A. plus some education credits
NEW JERSEY	60 semester hours college	Regular New Jersey teaching certificate

State		
NEW MEXICO	High school graduation	Regular New Mexico teaching certificate
NEW YORK	Bachelor's degree	Regular New York teaching certificate after 40 days
NORTH CAROLINA	60 semester hours college	Regular North Carolina teaching certificate
NORTH DAKOTA	Expired certification	Regular North Dakota teaching certificate
OHIO	120 semester hours college	Regular Ohio teaching certificate
OKLAHOMA	Bachelor's degree	Regular Oklahoma teaching certificate after 35 days
OREGON	Expired Oregon or non-Oregon certification	Regular Oregon teaching certificate
PENNSYLVANIA	Will waive certain incomplete certification requirements	Regular Pennsylvania teaching certificate

Chart I: CAN I QUALIFY? *(continued)*

State	Minimum Requirements	Long-term Requirements
RHODE ISLAND	Will waive certain incomplete certification requirements	Regular Rhode Island teaching certificate
SOUTH CAROLINA	90 semester hours college	90 semester hours college plus experience
SOUTH DAKOTA	Bachelor's degree	Regular South Dakota teaching certificate
TENNESSEE	Two years college	Two years college
TEXAS	90 semester hours college	90 semester hours college
UTAH	90 quarter hours of college	Regular Utah teaching certificate
VERMONT	Over 18 years of age	Regular Vermont teaching certificate
VIRGINIA	Bachelor's degree	Regular Virginia teaching certificate

State		
WASHINGTON	Bachelor's degree plus education credits for emergency; regular certification in some areas	Regular Washington teaching certificate
WEST VIRGINIA	Bachelor's degree plus training at county level in some areas	Regular West Virginia teaching certificate
WISCONSIN	Bachelor's degree	Regular Wisconsin teaching certificate
WYOMING	60 semester hours college	Regular Wyoming teaching certificate

3.

How Much Can I Earn?

Teaching will never make you rich; substitute teaching even less so. Few part-time occupations will, of course, unless you consider stunt driving (or have a penchant for picking the right horses).

But when you consider the relatively low-risk factor in subbing and the fact that it requires no capital outlay—and when you add to that the flexibility of hours and the respectability of the job—it begins to look even more attractive.

So if what you had in mind was the welcome addition of two or three hundred dollars per month, and maybe more, then you've come to the right place. In fact, depending upon where in the country you live, it is possible to earn four, five, even six hundred dollars or more for working eight to ten days every month!

Not bad, you say. But why the regional salary differences?

Actually, there are several factors in play here, not the least of which is the daily rate of pay. Most subs are paid on a per diem basis with checks issued once or twice each month. But the interesting fact about pay rates is the variance from one state to another.

From the same random sampling of school districts that yielded the standards for credential requirements nationwide, I also learned about current rates of pay. In a chart at the end of this chapter I list, state by state, the average daily compensation for substitutes in 1982. But before you peek, I would like to remind you of the following:

Insofar as it was possible to do so, I arrived at each state average by polling at least two school districts in each state; one in or near the capital city and one in an outlying area. Generally speaking, the higher figure reflects the larger city rate. Depending upon where in the state you live, the pay scale may be higher or lower.

Bear in mind that the figures may be augmented somewhat by recent cost of living increases or salary hikes in some areas.

Now you may peek, if you like. When you come back, we'll talk more about the rates as well as about the myriad other factors that will ultimately affect the size of your paycheck.

You undoubtedly checked your own state first and then jogged up and down the columns of numbers to see how it compares to other states. I told you it was interesting, didn't I?

Perhaps the best that can be said about the startling variances is that they probably reflect the general pay scales as well as the cost of living index in any given state.

In some cases they reflect, as well, the level of academic preparedness necessary to secure a credential. In other words, subs who are teaching with regular certification under their belts are earning more than subs who hold an "emergency," "provisional," or "substandard" credential.

Wherever two figures are shown for the state, the higher figure may represent either this more rigorous certification requirement or simply the difference between urban and suburban areas.

Remember, too, that the closer you live to a major city the higher the rate will be. This is partly because the inner city sub may have a tougher time than his country cousin and partly because pay rates in general are higher in the city than in the suburbs.

If there is a national average to be gleaned from the chart, it falls within the range of $30 to $40 per diem. Based on this, several states seem to stand head and shoulders above the rest while others lag sadly behind.

Why, you may ask, should I do the same day's work for $35 for which someone else is earning $60? Because, dear friends, things are not always what they seem to be, and sometimes there are compensating factors.

New York and California pay among the highest in the nation, although their highest figures represent long-term or "special" (that is, difficult) assignments. You must also remember that these are *averages*. Subs twenty miles outside the immediate Los Angeles inner city, for example, are paid considerably less than those within the city limits. The same holds true in New York.

Alaska follows closely behind these states. But the cost of living in Alaska is considerably higher than, say, in some of the midwestern states. Higher salaries are the norm.

West Virginia pays well. But in some areas it requires regular certification, narrowing the field from which it draws. In effect, the state pays more for more stringent qualifications.

The same may be said for Oregon and Washington, which offer higher salaries in return for stricter requirements. And again, the daily rate for subs in the Portland, Oregon, area is considerably higher than in the outlying areas of that state.

On the other hand, some states that seem to pay less will offer other compensations and benefits that must be taken into account.

Several states that fall within the low to median range of daily compensation offer subs the opportunity to join the state teachers' retirement program. If this benefit is of value to you in terms of your own retirement it must certainly be considered a bonus.

In Madison, Wisconsin, some subs are not only eligible for retirement benefits but they may also enroll in a group health insurance plan (for which they pay their own premium). If a group health insurance plan is not otherwise available to you, this can amount to substantial annual savings.

A specialized group of St. Louis, Missouri, subs (of whom we'll talk more later) is offered not only medical benefits but sick leave as well. This is a benefit rarely enjoyed by part-time employees of any kind and is surely worthy of consideration.

There are still other equalizing factors. Cedar Rapids, Iowa, and Louisville, Kentucky, provide really helpful substitute handbooks as well as good resource centers and some workshops. Birmingham, Alabama, while on the low end of the pay scale, also offers workshops that may well make your job easier.

Wayne County (Detroit area), Michigan, uses more than one thousand subs daily, greatly increasing your chances to work regularly. They offer added benefits to long-term subs.

Substitutes in Orlando, Florida, are paid in the median range—but ten consecutive days in one classroom constitutes long-term status, and the pay increases to that of the beginning full-time teacher. Alexandria, Virginia, uses one-third of its entire sub roster daily and offers substantial increases after the eleventh consecutive day.

All of these factors may in some way enhance the enjoyment of your part-time career and/or affect the size of your paycheck. When all is said and done, the sub who works ten days a month in a rural area for $35 per day will earn more money (and probably have an easier time of it) than the sub in the inner city who is called only five days per month at $50 per day. The per diem rate is one area that is strictly within the school district's control.

Another area that is beyond your control is the matter of need for substitutes. While you may wish to work ten or fifteen days each month, there is no way to guarantee that the district will require your services that frequently. Most of us are at the mercy of the district's daily need, which teeters back and forth based on such variables as illness, sick leave, and the number of regular teachers in the system.

An unusual situation exists in St. Louis, Missouri, where a specially trained group of subs who have Life Certification are *guaranteed* to work 80 percent of the school year. They are also eligible for the added benefits of which I spoke earlier.

But in return for this guaranteed 80 percent work time, these St. Louis subs must in turn guarantee the school district that they will be available 80 percent of the year. The key word here is *available*, for availability is one of the factors that does fall under your control and that can and will affect the size of your paycheck.

At the time you are hired by a particular school district you will be asked to list the days of the week on which you will be available to work. If you are enrolled in a college class on Mondays and Wednesdays or have any other such regular commitments, you may elect to make yourself available to the district only on Tuesdays, Thursdays, and Fridays. "If I can work three days a week," you say to yourself, "that's all I really need to do."

However, you have no assurance that the district will need you on those three days every week. It is important to realize that by limiting the number of days on which you are available, you may be severely limiting the number of days per month you will work for that district at all.

There are only some twenty possible working days in the

average school district month—sometimes fewer because of holidays. By limiting yourself to three days a week, or twelve per month, you may be greatly restricting your chances of being called. Unless your district badly needs subs and has a small roster from which to draw, the likelihood of your being needed on every day you are available is slim.

Most districts use their subs on the basis of simple rotation. Requests for a specific sub are filled first. Then subs are called alphabetically and in accordance with days available until all of the absences are filled. If the district has more than enough subs to meet current demand, your name will come up less frequently.

Be aware that if your goal is to work as many days each month as possible you must make yourself available five days per week. If you are satisfied to teach on a less regular basis, then you may choose to restrict your days of availability.

"Okay," you say. "I will rearrange my schedule to take night classes or whatever in order to be available more regularly." But what about those days when you simply have too many pressing things to do or your own sick child is home? Are you expected to say "yes" every morning that the sub clerk calls?

Of course not. In most cases the district realizes that if you wanted full-time work, you would have chosen it. Subbing is a part-time career and nobody will expect you to be available one hundred percent of the time. Even that selected group of St. Louis subs has a 20 percent leeway!

By all means, feel free to turn down a day's subbing for personal reasons. But do it judiciously. If you turn down assignments too often, you may find yourself being called less and less.

The sub clerk's job is not an easy one. He or she is on the spot to fill unexpected vacancies in the schools quickly and often at the last moment. Naturally, the clerk will

come to rely on those subs on the roster who are most re-
liable as well as on those who have a reputation for doing a
good job.

Another factor within your control that can affect the
size of your paycheck is the number of grade levels and
special classes in which you are willing to sub.

At the same time you are asked to specify the days on
which you can work, you will be asked your choice of
grades from kindergarten through high school. The greater
the flexibility you display in this area, the greater the likelihood of being called.

Chapter 7 deals specifically with the social and academic
differences between grade levels in the hope that you may
decide to try them all. You can always opt to restrict yourself later if you decide that the primaries are not your cup
of tea or that the high school level is more than you had
bargained for. In the beginning, at least, do try all the different grades. You may be in for some interesting sur-
prises.

The same may be said for trying special classes, such as
those for the hearing impaired or otherwise handicapped.
One of the most gratifying days I ever spent in a classroom
was with a group of deaf six and seven year olds. A
teacher's aide was present to help with communication. But
I learned a lot of sign language before the day was done,
and the motivation and zest for learning those kids dis-
played quickly overcame my initial hesitation.

Usually, a district will not assign you to such classes unless there is an aide or co-teacher to help. But your willingness to try is important to the schools, since these vacancies
are especially difficult to fill.

In short, the more flexibility you maintain, the more days
you will spend in a classroom. And the better the job you
do while there, the more often you will be requested.

If your calls are fewer than you'd hoped and it is geographically feasible, you may choose to register with another district as well in the hope that you will work more frequently. Be alert to the possibility of long-term assignments. Investigate your eligibility for them.

How much can you earn? It's a simple matter of arithmetic: the daily rate of pay times the number of days you work.

There is nothing you can do about the prevailing per diem rate or the number of daily absences within your district. But your own flexibility and topnotch performance can expand the size of your paycheck.

Chart II: HOW MUCH CAN I EARN?

State	Per Diem Rate	Additional Benefits
Alabama	$21–$25	Long-term only
Alaska	$63–75	None
Arizona	$32–40	None
Arkansas	$27–30	None
California	$44–86	Some optional retirement
Colorado	$35–50	Retirement
Connecticut	$30–40	None
District of Columbia	$35–55	None
Delaware	$25–45	None
Florida	$25–35	Long-term only
Georgia	$24–30	None
Hawaii	$44–52	None
Idaho	$25–35	None
Illinois	$25–35	None
Indiana	$30–35	None
Iowa	$38–43	Long-term only
Kansas	$40–50	None
Kentucky	$25–55	None
Louisiana	$25–35	None

State	Per Diem Rate	Additional Benefits
Maine	$27–40	Retirement
Maryland	$25–45	Long-term only
Massachusetts	$25–55	Long-term only
Michigan	$40–60	Long-term only
Minnesota	$45–55	Optional retirement
Mississippi	$30–65	None
Missouri	$25–63	Long-term only
Montana	$30–40	Long-term only
Nebraska	$35–46	None
Nevada	$45–60	None
New Hampshire	$30–40	None
New Jersey	$25–45	None
New Mexico	$28–44	None
New York	$35–93	Optional retirement
North Carolina	$30–35	None
North Dakota	$40–45	Long-term only
Ohio	$30–40	Long-term only
Oklahoma	$25–42	None
Oregon	$40–65	Limited retirement
Pennsylvania	$32–50	Some after one year
Rhode Island	$22–35	None
South Carolina	$26–34	Optional Retirement
South Dakota	$30–40	None
Tennessee	$30–50	None
Texas	$35–40	None
Utah	$25–66	Limited retirement
Vermont	$25–35	None
Virginia	$42–56	None
Washington	$40–55	None
West Virginia	$50–60	Long-term only
Wisconsin	$35–66	Retirement
Wyoming	$30–40	Long-term only

4.

Where Do I Begin?

By now you have determined that you are not only interested in subbing but that you are quite possibly qualified to be a substitute teacher in your community. Where do you begin?

Start with your local school district. A telephone call to the district office will establish the current need for subs in your area. Unless your community is far different from the norm, they will be happy to answer your inquiry.

The best time to make your call is in late summer or early fall when the new term is getting underway. However, with the need for subs as greaas it is, you can double-check the educational requirements and probably set an appointment to be interviewed at any mutually agreeable time.

If you live in a large city you will most likely interview for a single school district that serves a broad metropolitan area, staffing many schools. In the suburbs you may have several districts from which to choose since many small cities and townships operate independent school systems.

Your credential will be issued by the state in which you live and will allow you to substitute teach in any school district within that state. To start with, choose the one that is closest to your home. Ultimately, you may work for more than one district at a time.

Take with you to the interview a copy of your diploma and, more important, a transcript of your school records. If you have ever held a teaching credential of any type, even one that has expired or was issued by another state, take that with you as well.

In scheduling your appointment, the district personnel may ask that you bring a copy of your birth certificate or proof of American citizenship. And before you can be hired you may need to have a physical exam, blood tests, or tuberculosis screening.

Be prepared, at the time of the interview, to make the most of all your qualifications. Apart from any diplomas or credentials you may have and no matter how many units of college credit you have satisfactorily completed, the interviewer will want to know that you have had some experience in working with children.

If you have taught in the past, the evidence is obvious. But what about those of you who have never faced a classroom full of students?

Have you ever been a scout leader? A camp counselor? A dance instructor? Have you taught arts and crafts at a youth center? Coached a Little League team? Conducted tours through the children's museum?

Have you volunteered your time as a teacher's aide? Have you tutored? Chaperoned field trips?

Bring to mind anything in your past work or volunteer experience that relates to your supervision of children or young adults. If you have raised four kids and half the neighborhood has camped out in your backyard (or your kitchen!) mention that, too. Anything that indicates that you have had the opportunity to deal with large groups is a point in your favor.

You may be asked how you feel about discipline; how you might handle a sticky situation like a fight between two children or a child who flouts your authority. Trust your instincts and be honest and practical in responding to such questions. In most cases, there are no right or wrong answers. You are simply presenting yourself as a mature individual who can meet new situations and make decisions comfortably.

The interviewer will want to know about your special skills and interests. To sub at the junior high or high school level you need to be proficient in specific subject areas. At the elementary school level, what can you bring with you to the classroom to make you an interesting teacher? Here again, you need not be modest about your accomplishments or your experience.

If you speak a foreign language, play a musical instrument, or direct a local glee club, your services may be very much in demand. These talents relate to specialized areas of teaching for which substitutes are very hard to find.

Similarly, if you know sign language, are adept at calisthenics or at staging theatrical productions, or have any other distinctive areas of expertise, the school district may need you more than you know.

If you have traveled extensively or have an unusual hobby or collection, you have much to share with your students. Can you draw? Sew? Use a jigsaw? Teach a jig? If so, you have a built-in advantage.

Take stock of what it is that makes you uniquely you. It is *you* you are selling to the school district. And don't be discouraged if your skills and experience don't seem enormous or unusual. We will devote a later chapter to helping you learn to use your own special talents in the classroom. For now, take pride in whatever you do well and in your willingness to share it with others.

As a result of your interview the personnel director will determine your qualifications for the job and can pinpoint any requirements you may need to fulfill before the paper-work process can begin. If you are eligible to sub you may be able to begin as soon as your qualifications have been verified, even though it may take several weeks or months before your actual credential is issued. The fee required for credential application varies from state to state.

Before you apply for the necessary credential or accept a position on the spot, there are several questions you may want answered to feel confident in your decision.

The daily pay rate is important, of course, although it is not arguable. The compensation is set by the district and it is what it is, like it or not. However, if you have a choice of districts, you may find that the pay rate varies considerably within a relatively small geographic area.

In Los Angeles, for example, subs are currently paid up to $80 per day for some assignments. In suburban districts some twenty to forty miles away the daily rate drops to somewhere between $45 and $60. You may or may not wish to drive the extra miles and take on the challenge of the inner city. But you certainly do have the choice be-tween working for the district nearest your home or the one ten miles away that pays more.

Remember that your credential is issued by the state. You may apply for it through any district in the state but are permitted to sub anywhere once you have it. By all means, contact any district within a reasonable distance and compare the salaries and benefits.

In the end, however, it may not be the daily rate upon which you base your decision. The more important ques-tion may be: how many days per month can you reasonably expect to teach? In areas where the demand for subs is great you will probably work more often. Working eight days a month at $60 per day may be far more attractive than four days a month at a higher rate.

How many subs are currently employed in the district in which you are interviewing? What is the average number of days per month that most of them are working? Bear in mind that really good subs are requested frequently and work more often. Hopefully, you will become one of these—and in very short order! But in the beginning it helps to know something about the district's projection of how often you may be called.

Does the district offer any training for subs? Is there an orientation? A procedures book? It is precisely because there is such a dearth of training that this book was written in the first place. Still, if your district offers any help pertaining specifically to its own schools, for heaven's sake take advantage of it!

You may be given a choice of those grade levels for which you prefer to sub. Apart from our discussions of them, one way to become familiar with their differences (and to get a sneak preview of your job) is to ask to be allowed to sit in on some classes before you begin to teach.

Most schools have no objection to visitors in the classroom. Teachers and students are accustomed to occasional visits by parents, aides, student teachers, and school officials. With permission from the district and/or principals, you can choose to spend some time observing primary (K–3), upper elementary (4–6), junior high, or high school classes.

Be prepared to find vast differences between one classroom and another, even within the same grade level. The students' abilities will vary, for one thing. For another, teachers, like all of us, have distinct personalities that are reflected in the way they teach.

Some rooms may seem like organized bedlam, the teacher animated, the children working busily and noisily in small, seemingly disconnected groups. It takes skill and practice to work efficiently in this kind of setting, but many teachers handle it admirably, getting peak performance from each group without losing sight of the whole.

While classrooms like this are lots of fun, we suggest you do not try to emulate them. Even experienced teachers can lose control and are subject to bouts of disorganization. The beginning sub has enough to learn without inviting chaos.

Other classrooms are quiet and orderly, with strict rules enforced in an atmosphere of much more formal learning. The teacher speaks softly, the children know what is expected of them, the work proceeds calmly and smoothly.

Of course there are all manner of classrooms in between, as you will note in your own observations. Don't be confused or put off by the differences you see. Accept it as confirmation that every teacher develops individual techniques based on personality, experience, and goals.

As you visit, make mental notes of any methods you might wish to borrow or build on. The various ways in which experienced teachers handle even such simple routines as bathroom calls can have an impact on the way you will do things.

One teacher we know uses a system of having her students hold up one finger if they wish to sharpen a pencil, two fingers to request a drink of water, and three fingers if they wish to visit the restroom. A nod from the teacher means permission granted, yet the entire exchange is silent and disturbs no one's work or concentration.

Much can be learned by observing other teachers deal with chatterboxes, test correction, clean-up chores. When combined with your own ideas and resourcefulness, the things you see will help you to develop those methods that work best for you.

Every school district uses standardized textbooks for each subject, grade level, and school. As you visit sample classrooms, browse through the textbooks in use. Unless you have a mind like a computer you will never store away their content. But you will begin to fathom at what age simple math gives way to compound fractions, and nutrition to dissection of frogs.

You may also have the opportunity to glance at the teacher's editions of these same textbooks, which provide answers and teaching tips and will do a lot to reassure you that you do not have to be Albert Einstein to teach a seventh grade science class.

Pay attention to what goes on in the lunchroom, on the playground, in the corridors. As a sub, you will have to serve duty in these areas. You may note that every school has an ambiance all its own, with differing ways of teaching children about sportsmanship, self-control, and citizenship. Yet the basic goals are universal, and it will help to have a glimmering of what is expected without having to ask too many questions.

All in all, two or three days spent observing classroom activity will benefit you in more ways than one. First, you will get a clear idea of what's going on in schools today and how you will fit into the picture. Second, you will be introduced to teachers and principals you might otherwise have never met.

When teachers find themselves unable to report for work it is their responsibility to let the school district know in time for a substitute to be called. Sometimes, as happens when several teachers will be attending a workshop, it is the principal who calls the district office for the subs. In either case the caller may ask for "a sub" in general or may specifically request Mr. Jones or Mrs. Green if he or she is available.

Teachers and principals who respect a particular sub's capabilities are inclined to request that sub. If you have spent some time in their classrooms and are familiar with the work and the students, the requested sub could be you.

Certainly the fact that you invested your time in unpaid observation in order to prepare yourself for subbing speaks highly of your diligence and initiative.

It never hurts to "know somebody," and these first introductions could provide a valuable stepping-off point for you in your new career.

Once you have definitely decided to sub and have applied for the necessary credential, feel free to contact any friends who are teachers and let them know of your new substitute status. Stop by the school your own children attended and tell them of your availability too. And what about the teacher whose class you visited last year as an "expert" on spelunking or decoupage?

You may be tempted to check in with several neighboring school districts regarding their need for subs in an effort to get your new career off the ground.

I offer the following word of caution. Your subbing career may be slow to start. As a newcomer you will need to prove yourself to the district. Your phone may ring less frequently than you'd hoped. Rest assured that in the normal course of things you will be called more and more. And if you have registered to sub in several districts at once, it can be downright annoying if not actually hairraising to have your phone ring three or four times between six and six-fifteen A.M.!

Be willing to start slowly while you gain your experience and, like the proverbial tortoise, get ready for a big, successful finish.

5.

A Look at Today's Classroom

Times have changed since you were in school. Whether you remember the strict, conforming classrooms of the forties and fifties; the changing, turbulent schools of the sixties; or the experimental, open classrooms of the seventies, you may be sure that the picture has changed as the face of America has changed.

PHYSICAL CHANGES

One marked difference many of you may notice is in the physical layout of modern schools. In some urban areas the old, multistoried buildings are still in use. In suburbia, however, where school construction is newer, the tendency is toward single stories (with outdoor corridors in mild climates) and banks of windows all around.

Bright colors, natural light, and a feeling of spaciousness provide a cheerful atmosphere in which to learn. Classrooms are individualized through the use of bulletin boards, artwork, graphics, and other accessories that reflect the interests and emphasis of the teacher and the students.

Articles of room decor, nature-study projects, murals and plants are often a source of pride (and information) to the children, who will vie for the privilege of feeding Mrs. Edwards' goldfish when she is absent or changing the date on Mr. Lerner's outsized calendar.

If you sub in a room where live plants or animals abound, check for the monitors who have the current responsibility for their care. Students usually rotate in these jobs, and you will undoubtedly hear a chorus of protests if you allow some tricky interloper to usurp anyone's chore.

In many newer schools the lunchroom often serves double duty as an auditorium or gymnasium. A multipurpose area with tables and benches that fold away against the walls when not in use, the lunchroom may be used for school assemblies, dances or, on rainy days, athletics and games.

DRESS CODES

The dress code in many areas has changed drastically in recent years. Those of us who remember wearing white shirts and ties to school or having our hemlines measured to see that they were no shorter than the prescribed number of inches from the floor may be surprised to find that shorts and sandals are acceptable attire in hot weather and that the length of a student's hair is entirely his own business.

The teacher's dress code has been similarly altered. While we are expected to be neatly dressed and well-groomed, women often wear slacks and pants suits and men casual slacks and sport shirts.

A visit to your local school will show what attire is *de rigueur* in your area. Bear in mind, however, that the sub who is dressed in a more formal manner may command more respect, at least initially, than the one whose clothes are ultracasual.

THE STUDENTS

Today's students are a different breed. For one thing, they have grown up in a world of television. Beginning with "Sesame Street" and continuing with an exposure to police stories, soap operas, and comedic innuendo, they arrive at kindergarten far more worldly than youngsters of past generations.

Whatever your feelings about children and television in terms of its educational values, there is little doubt that today's students enter school with an awareness and a diversity of information that most of us acquired much later in life. For better or worse they are more knowing in their attitudes, more advanced in their thinking, and more independent in their behavior.

This does not mean, necessarily, that they are better equipped with the rudiments of learning. Muppets notwithstanding, the variety of these children's experiences does not insure that they have memorized the alphabet or are familiar with colors and numbers.

Statistics remind us repeatedly that more women work outside the home today than in any preceding generation. More and more children move up to kindergarten from a background of day care or nursery school. They are bringing with them varying degrees of academic readiness, emotional stability, and social know-how. When you start with a group this divergent, you must develop ways to deal with the differences.

As in so many areas of modern American life, we are teaching in an era of specialization. Sophisticated testing methods rapidly identify intellectually gifted children and students with learning disabilities. Those with learning disabilities are further categorized as physically impaired, emotionally handicapped, educably mentally retarded, and so forth.

School systems are developing appropriate programs to better serve the needs of these children. Some students are assigned to permanent classrooms with specially trained teachers. Others are assigned to regular classrooms but attend special classes for a number of hours per week.

Regular teachers are aware of the particular problems and capabilities of these exceptional students. The sub does not have this advantage. It takes skill and perception to recognize that the boy who refuses to read for you suffers from dyslexia or that the girl who cannot stay in her seat is truly hyperkinetic and is not merely out to try your patience. It is a skill many subs develop only with time and experience.

WORKABLE DISCIPLINE

Behavior problems that result from physical or emotional disorders are relatively rare. Yet teachers must cope with them and they are generally aware that common approaches to discipline don't always work with these children. A certain amount of extra patience is required.

Also, it is precisely this type of child who finds it most difficult to accept a substitute teacher or any change in his routine. His ordinarily difficult behavior may become even more outrageous in your presence.

We hesitate to advise you to turn a deaf ear when you're not entirely sure what you're facing. But if you suspect that you are not dealing with an average child, don't attempt average kinds of discipline. Don't call attention to his every transgression. React only to what seems severe. And be prepared to ask for help from the office (that is, having him removed) if his behavior becomes unduly disruptive or threatening to anyone in class.

As for the wiseacres and plain old garden-variety mischief makers, well, teachers through the ages have had to deal with problem children, long before anyone heard of hyperkinesis. What has changed is that the knuckle rapping and posterior slapping once administered with impunity to "deserving" students is nowadays strictly forbidden.

Corporal punishment by teachers is not only taboo in most areas, it can even be grounds for dismissal. Educators, therefore, have had to devise new and practical methods for keeping classroom behavior under control.

"Assertive discipline," a term very much in vogue, is a method by which various consequences are meted out in accordance with the student's infractions. Most often, if a child misbehaves, his name is listed on the blackboard. This acts as a warning. If he errs again, a check is placed next to his name. One check may earn detention, two checks a visit to the principal, three checks the telephoning of his parents, and so on up to and including suspension for the most serious offenses.

The child is expected to accept responsibility for his own actions and assertive discipline clearly defines the limits. It is a widely used system of which you will want to be aware.

The other side of the coin is "positive reinforcement." This technique stresses rewarding students for good behavior and achievements. When you read about "Superstars" in Chapter 10 you will recognize it as a tool for positive reinforcement. Names of good workers are listed on the blackboard and similarly checked, with such rewards offered as ten minutes free time, early recess, or sometimes even small gifts that the teacher or sub has accrued for just this purpose. Pencils, erasers, posters, and the like are examples. You will surely find sources of free materials in your own home town. Used sparingly but consistently, this simple reward system can be highly effective with children.

Warning: Do not be tempted to use candy or gum as rewards or prizes. Chewing gum is forbidden on most campuses. Candy causes tooth decay. Last but not least, you will not want to be hailed in the parking lot by some chubby third grader with a very loud voice as the "lollipop lady" or the "candy man." Be discerning if you decide to use gifts.

In the average classroom a combination of assertive discipline and positive reinforcement, in one form or another, should be all you need to elicit cooperation and good spirits from your students. Read more about "Superstars" and "Sour Apples" in Chapter 10.

TEACHING METHODS

While much of the same information we learned as children is still being taught in schools today, the methods of teaching it have changed somewhat.

Textbooks, of course, will never go out of style. But there is far greater use of audiovisual materials, including our old friend, television. Public television and local educational channels are regular visitors to today's classrooms with programs that teach language, science, and history for young children.

You may find programmed teaching machines which students can use independently, keeping score of their own achievements. Progress is supervised by the teacher, but the machines allow youngsters to proceed at their own individual pace, using film strips, charts, and study guides.

Most school districts have educational film libraries augmented by films distributed by business and industry. When a teacher knows in advance that he or she will be absent, a film may be ordered for the substitute's use. If you have had no experience with sixteen millimeter sound projectors, we suggest you visit your local school resource center and learn how to use one. Many older children know how to operate these projectors and vie for the privilege of doing so in the classroom. In the primary grades, however, you will need to be the chief engineer.

There is widespread use of duplicated materials known as "dittoes." Available for every topic from reading comprehension to map study to color-by-number art projects, stacks of dittoes are kept by many teachers in their classrooms either for regular study or to be used as timefillers or for extra credit.

Sometimes the teacher will keep in the desk a "sub folder" that includes some of these duplicated materials, and will suggest that the sub use them as needed to round out the day.

CURRICULUM

For the most part, curriculum is standardized in the sense that all fourth graders in the state study a particular phase of history, math, or science, as do all second graders and all sixth graders. Thus, once you have become familiar with the material covered in a particular grade level, you will meet much of the same material in the same grade level no matter where in the district you sub.

Workbooks are a dandy adjunct to the textbook. A lesson is introduced and explained by the teacher (or sub) using the appropriate text. Each child has a softcover workbook in which he does exercises pertaining to the topic just covered. The work performed in this manner is evaluated and gives an excellent indication of whether or not the lesson has been learned.

If there is a teacher's edition of the textbook, there will be a teacher's edition of the workbook as well. Use it to help you correct the student's work.

In the traditional or self-contained classroom all of the

work is supervised and maintained by one teacher. Children may be grouped according to their level of achievement but one teacher handles all the groups. Subbing in a class like this means that you will decide how and when each lesson is to be taught and whether or not to involve the entire class.

Some schools use an open classroom or team teaching approach, wherein the class is exposed to two or three teachers every day who teach their own "specialties" in math, language, or science. This type of classroom structure sometimes involves moving students from one room to another.

If you are assigned to a team teaching situation your lesson plan should reflect it. You may depend upon the other teachers involved to let you know when the students will change rooms and what material is to be taught.

COPING WITH IT ALL

Today's classroom is a vital, individual learning center with a culture all of its own. It is made up of students with various backgrounds, attitudes, and achievement levels and is supervised by a teacher who puts his or her own stamp or personality into play.

It has changed in style, scope, and methodology in the many ways we've mentioned here. But some things, it seems, never change. In every class there are the ingroups and the outcasts, the manipulators and the scapegoats, the quick-to-learn and the couldn't-care-less.

As a substitute, you cannot possibly know the children's abilities and problems as the regular teacher does. You cannot be expected to perform each task in the same way that their teacher does or to make decisions about study groups and discipline with quite the same expertise.

But you can be alert to the climate of a class, to its mood

or general ambiance. You will strive for cheerfulness and tact, accepting each child at face value. In fact, there is a certain advantage in not knowing who the troublemakers are.

I tell my students, when I introduce the Superstars list, "You people know who the superstars are in this class and who are the ones who get into trouble. Don't tell me. I don't want to know. I am new to your class and to me you are all superstars until you prove to me otherwise. So this is your chance to put your best foot forward—no matter what happened yesterday."

By having everyone start out on an equal footing, by making consistent decisions based on what you see *today*, by being open-minded and flexible with regard to class structure, and by *expecting* to enjoy yourself, you'll put your own best foot forward toward understanding today's classroom and being a Supersub.

6.

Choosing the Grade Level for Me

You don't need me to tell you that kids at any age are at once a joy and a frustration. When my own were very young, friends used to say, "Enjoy them while they're little. The bigger the kids, the bigger the problems."

As a parent I've discovered that in many ways this is so. When they're small they're docile and placid and sweet and Mother and Daddy know best. The more independence the children find, the more they argue and question and test and the more clashes ensue.

On the other hand, I rather enjoy their questions and sometimes even their arguments. I marvel at their growing perception of the world and their search for their own place in it.

As a teacher I've found that my feelings about students are startlingly similar to my feelings about my own children. I adore those darling kindergarteners with their cowlicks and little starched petticoats. They're still docile and placid and sweet. But my greatest joy comes from the fifth and sixth graders who argue and question and test.

Perhaps it is because of some curious quirk in my own personality, for there are many subs who look at me askance. Why subject yourself to the upper graders when the little ones are so trusting? So innocent and eager to please?

Because, for me, as thrilling as it is to watch a child learn to read, it is somehow more thrilling to watch him stretch his mind—to make sense out of fragments and logic out of the words he long ago learned how to read. I enjoy it even though it means more attention to discipline and more challenge in keeping him busy.

The purpose of this chapter, then, is to help you get familiar with the differences between one grade level and another. We will talk about behavior, about attitudes and expectations, and about the academics involved.

We'll take a little look at what makes *you* tick: at the curious quirks in *your* personality that may lead you to prefer one group over another.

I cannot urge you strongly enough, at least in the beginning of your career, to try your hand at subbing in all the grade levels from kindergarten through high school. Each has its challenges and its own rewards and since you may be subbing in a different classroom each day, variety will add spice to your life. In addition, as I have previously pointed out, the more grade levels you are willing to teach, the more you are likely to work.

In most school districts the grade levels are divided into primary (kindergarten through third), upper elementary (fourth through sixth), junior high, and high schools. For our purposes we will break them down even further, for the differences are notable indeed.

KINDERGARTEN

The venerable Dr. Benjamin Spock, without whose meticulous descriptions of rashes and fevers I could never have raised my own children, describes the typical five year old as affectionate and agreeable, wanting to emulate and please.

Nowhere is this more apparent than in a roomful of kindergarten children. Reluctant though some of them may have been to leave home, they soon adjust to the world of school with eager and boundless enthusiasm.

They are cheerful, energetic, anxious to please, and accepting—even worshipful—of their teachers. They can accept a substitute with as much equanimity as they accept a babysitter at home, and they are open to your friendliness and ideas.

But they are usually sensitive and sometimes fearful—of everything from rejection to cloudbursts. You must be prepared to deal with "He smudged my new shoe!" and with wails of "I'm afraid in the dark!"

They are extremely susceptible to reactions from their peers. I once subbed in a kindergarten class on a day that was something of a phenomenon, at least in Southern California. In the midst of our normally drippy but mannerly rainy season, we had a thunderstorm of truly classic proportions. Lightning flashed and thunder crashed in a display most unusual for our area.

One or two children began to whimper a bit and it wasn't long before their fears took hold and spread to the other puzzled youngsters. In a matter of moments they tumbled forward, pell-mell. My arms were simply not large enough!

With sudden inspiration (or maybe desperation) I began to sing "I Whistle a Happy Tune" from *The King and I,* which says, "Whenever I feel afraid, I hold my head erect . . ."

This so arrested the children's attention that I was able to seat them in a circle at my feet and to teach them the words of the song. Fortunately, our thunderstorm was short-lived and we spent what was left of the morning talking about rain and where it comes from and what makes thunder and lightning.

The point of all this is that kindergarteners require a special sort of patience and affection and more than a little imagination. They respond quickly and wholeheartedly to whatever is presented to them, for many are still babies at heart.

Academically, they may range quite a bit. Typically, there are a few who are reading while others do not yet know the alphabet. They work on letter, number, and word recognition, on printing, and on counting groups of numbers. Music, art, games, and creative play are very much a part of their curriculum.

If you are comfortable with young children, are cheerful and patient, and particularly if you tell a good story or play a musical instrument, you will be happy subbing in kindergarten. Whether or not there is a teacher's lesson plan available you will find it easy to present interesting and creative lessons for their developmental growth.

And even if, as I do, you prefer the challenge of an older group, there is nothing like a day in the innocent and loving atmosphere of a kindergarten classroom to restore your faith in humanity!

FIRST, SECOND, AND THIRD GRADES

First graders have outgrown their shyness and some of their keen sensitivity. At one stage or another they are learning to read and print and to do simple addition. History is now a part of their curriculum as they study, for instance, the reasons behind our holidays.

They are learning to be organized in their work habits and they set great store by the routines and schedules that are part of their classroom life. They regard their teachers with affection and respect and are most eager to help the sub learn their daily routine and fit into their neat little world.

First graders take a great deal of pride in their work and in themselves and their families. They love to "share" (as in "Show and Tell") books, seashells, or other interesting objects from home. So much so, in fact, that it is not unusual for a youngster to volunteer to share—and then stand, empty-handed and tongue-tied, until he finally "remembers" a new belt buckle or a filling in his tooth!

Lesson plans are easy to supplement since story-telling, simple art projects, and pantomimes are well-received educational timefillers.

Second and third graders are "old hands" at school. They are well organized and respectful, although they are now somewhat more concerned with what their peers think of them than they were a year or two ago.

Most are reading well and doing addition, subtraction, and some multiplication tables. They work on spelling and the rudiments of sentence construction. They study health and nature, learning about nutrition and growth. State history may be part of their curriculum, as well as American history through study about presidents and historical events.

Second and third graders are cheerful, friendly, and energetic. They are open to your ideas and suggestions and are very receptive to art projects, pantomimes, or other acting exercises, sports, and stories.

Most classrooms at this age level are stocked with storybooks and activities. A quick trek through Part Three of this book will give you lots of ideas for games that make learning fun for these fun-loving six, seven, and eight year olds.

Many subs prefer teaching in the primaries because of the easygoing and uncomplicated atmosphere. The children are generally well behaved and are sticklers for rules and conventions.

FOURTH GRADE

Fourth grade is a transitional period; an age when students are beginning to feel their oats. No longer considered primaries, they are not quite accepted by the more sophisticated fifth and sixth graders either. As a consequence they tend to clown around a lot and otherwise draw attention to themselves. Fortunately, they still have a healthy respect for authority that makes them fall into line.

Academically they are doing multiplication and division, preparing for decimals and fractions. Social studies are now more diverse, combining history, geography, and current events. They study grammar and punctuation, and probably have moved from printing to cursive handwriting. They are expected to read and do book reports, and are getting more homework than they have ever had before.

Fourth graders are athletic and curious, interested in the world around them. They have sharpened their abstract thinking skills, making this a wonderful age to begin using more complicated brainteasers and logic puzzles (see Part Three).

Reading aloud is still popular here, although the students at this age have outgrown simple storybooks. It's a good idea for the sub to keep a small stock of minimysteries and short stories for filling in odd moments at this level (see Appendix B for suggestions).

Sports and all sorts of learning games, art projects, and

play reading are excellent choices for supplementary activities. These kids are game to try anything and Part Three will keep your bag of tricks filled.

FIFTH AND SIXTH GRADES

Fifth and sixth graders are at the top of the heap in the elementary school setting and don't they know it! They're trying their wings in more ways than one, though they are perhaps less rambunctious in schools which continue through eighth grade.

They are aware of the physical changes that are taking place in them, and while some are becoming shyer with the opposite sex, others are becoming more aggressive. In any case, they are more keenly interested in acceptance by their peers than in impressing the sub with good behavior.

Alas, they have learned to be devious and manipulative and will tell you with wide-eyed innocence that Mrs. So-and-so *always* dismisses them early or that Rubik's Cubes are perfectly acceptable during study periods. You will need to be firm and decisive with this age group and to trust your own best judgment, while maintaining unflappable cordiality. This is the age when Superstars and other disciplinary ploys must be brought to bear. The children must be given some impetus to respect you and some confidence in your ability to control.

On the other hand these little "twerps" are quick-minded and versatile, often with remarkably adult perceptions and capabilities. For this reason, Brainteasers and Timefillers (as set forth in Part Three) become marvelous tools for all their guise of simply being fun.

These eleven and twelve year olds will respond to your naturalness and candor and to your treatment of them as young adults rather than as children. Their noisy effervescence will be more easily quelled by flicking the light switches than by attempting to speak over their voices. They will happily accept "jobs," such as collecting papers or helping to run the projector, that enhance their somewhat shaky self-esteem.

Academically they are often at different levels of achievement, some still struggling for mastery of the basics while others are reaching hard toward junior high. In math, for example, which now becomes preparatory to algebra and geometry, there will be some who have not yet memorized the times tables.

Their writing skills also are sharply divergent, making this an excellent age to use creative writing as an exercise in grammar and punctuation as well as literature. You may want to keep a stock of topic sentences in mind, such as "If I could be anything in the whole world," or "One dark and stormy night . . ."

Children at this level are learning to do long-term research projects involving encyclopedias and reference books. Take advantage of their natural competitiveness by assigning them to small teams that can "win" by coming up with answers to questions you pose.

The wise sub will choose classic short stories for filling in spare times, and use them as a springboard for debates, discussions, or role playing. Fifth and sixth graders are full of emotions and opinions, and welcome the opportunity to let steam escape through such organized and creative activities. Again, refer to Part Three for specific ideas in these areas.

Whether you are correcting a penmanship slant or teaching the reduction of fractions, helping to tie shoelaces or directing a research project, some factors remain constant in subbing for the K–6 levels.

You are responsible for every aspect of the classroom day from the flag salute through each subject area including physical education and the arts. You are the science teacher, the softball coach, the art director, and the resident expert on trivia. In other words, you are a well-rounded individual who is very, very flexible.

Since the same children are in your charge all day, you are the timekeeper as well. You keep the day moving from lesson to lesson, filling in when necessary with interesting and varied activities.

In the junior high and high school settings, your job is somewhat different. Chapter 11 will familiarize you with your responsibilities at those levels. For now, let's talk for a bit about the social and emotional differences in these older students and what you as a substitute may expect.

JUNIOR HIGH

Seventh and eighth graders are undergoing perhaps the greatest transition in all of their school years. Still in varying stages of physical development and emotional growth, the poor things are neither fish nor fowl.

They have left the well-known and secure world of elementary school behind them for the scary milieu of changing classes, intensified work, and budding social awareness. Surely they are not children. But they are light years away from those svelte and knowing high schoolers whom they try so hard to emulate.

Because they are unsure of themselves they can be difficult for the sub to handle. They may be loud, rude, flighty, or disorganized, and they require firmness, patience, and tact.

But in the junior high setting, the teacher is responsible for only one or two areas of their education. You will face a new group every hour and deal only with a specific subject. If your background or expertise is in science and you have forgotten how to diagram a sentence, stay away from English classes. The students will delight in your confusion.

If you know your subject matter, and if you are friendly but firm and keep your own feathers unruffled, there is no reason why you cannot maintain order.

Remember that these are children—for all their seeming sophistication—and that, like all children who are in a period of transition, they need acceptance and direction. If you have some familiarity with adolescent behavior, if you can see through the brittle veneer to the budding adults underneath and like them in spite of themselves, you can be a great junior high school sub.

HIGH SCHOOL

Most high school students have bridged the gap between adolescence and young adulthood. Though far from being fully matured, they are at least beginning to know who they are and what they want out of life.

While they are deeply concerned with popularity and the normal teen-age pursuits, many strive seriously toward college and career preparation. Others, alas, are merely marking time until the magic age of eighteen when they no longer have to go to school.

The mechanics of school—changing classes, consulting with counselors, research and testing—are no longer mysterious. They know what is expected of them and they will choose to follow the rules—or not.

The consequences for breaking the rules in high school are clear. Treat your students with friendly encouragement as young adults capable of performing properly. Don't hesitate to serve up the consequences if necessary.

As a substitute you must be knowledgeable about your subject. This is in-depth study, not basics or generality. You will almost always have a lesson plan, but if you do not the students can be instructed to read for this class or another or to catch up on homework or research.

In some ways subbing at the high school level can be as easy or as difficult as you make it. Chapter 11 will show you why this is so, and why many subs, particularly those with backgrounds rich in specific subject areas, prefer the high school setting for its objectivity, fast pace, and more adult milieu.

7.

Learning Basic Procedures

A substitute in California told me recently, "The first day I ever walked into a classroom as a sub I was full of confidence and good cheer. I knew I could do a good job and I wasn't particularly afraid of making a mistake. Then I picked up the roll sheet to take attendance and I stopped short. It suddenly occurred to me that I didn't know how to mark it! Was I supposed to use an X to indicate an absence? A check? A zero?

"I stared at it a moment feeling all the confidence drain out of me. I finally made a decision, of course, and stuck to it right or wrong. But that silly little minute really shook me up. It pointed up so graphically just how much I didn't know!"

Anyone who's ever been put in a position of authority without fully understanding the rules of the game can sympathize with that poor sub. There is nothing like one's own insecurity to undermine confidence. In a subbing situation, that sinking feeling that the kids know more than you do can really put you on the defensive.

There is nothing wrong with asking questions, certainly, or with admitting a little lack of knowledge. That same sub would probably never hesitate to ask, "Where does your teacher keep the art supplies?" or "Are you supposed to use ink or pencil?" But when it comes to basic procedures, like taking the roll or supervising a fire drill, it is important to feel that you do know the rules and that you are somehow in control.

Every school district—and sometimes every school within the district—has its own way of doing certain things. Lunch procedures, for example, or the movement of students from one area to another, may vary according to the principal's discretion. But many operations, like roll taking or fire drilling, are standardized within the district and fall under the heading of basic operating procedures. The same can be said of the paperwork in subbing—reporting hours, payroll duties, and the like.

The first and most obvious way to learn these basics is to pore through any substitute handbooks or district policy manuals that are available to you. While many of these will not give you a clue as to how to be a good sub, most will include the following important data:

- A map of the district and/or a list of school addresses, telephone numbers, principals, and secretaries. This will allow you to find your work location quickly and efficiently without taking the time of the sub clerk at the busy hour of six A.M. Addressing the principal and secretary by their names will make you feel more a part of the school.

- A summary of the substitute calling and report procedure. This will explain how teachers advise the district of impending absences and the basis on which substitutes are called. It should spell out your responsibility in accepting and refusing assignments and advising the sub clerk's office of your availability. In most areas a twenty-four hour electronic phone answering device is used to record messages to which the sub clerk can respond at six A.M.

• Class hours and bell schedules. Sometimes, because of school bus routing or for other reasons, the starting and closing schedules for schools within the district may vary. You will need to know the hours you will be expected to work at each school and the time and method of checking in.

• Time reporting and payroll information. Every district has its own method for keeping track of the number of days or partial days the substitute has worked. Hours must be carefully recorded and submitted to the district office at specific times each month if you are to receive your paycheck on time.

Pay periods should be clearly spelled out so that you can keep accurate records. Deductions made for social security, workman's compensation, optional retirement, or other benefits should be explained as well as salary step increments or long-term pay increases that may apply.

The same policy manual or substitute handbook *may* include the following:

• District policy for reporting emergencies. In the event that a student suffers an accident or illness while under your supervision, quick steps must be taken to insure prompt assistance and safety. By following the correct procedure you are helping to reduce the school's liability as well. It is important to understand and remember these procedures so that you can remain calm and capable should the need arise.

• Bell system for emergencies and drills. Fire and air raid drills are common to every school district. Disaster drills, such as those for earthquakes or tornadoes, may apply to certain areas. Often, you will be alerted if a drill is to take place on the day you are teaching. Nevertheless, it is crucial that you can distinguish between warning bells (two short bells for fire drill, three for air raid drill, for instance) so that you can lead your class quickly and efficiently.

• Drill procedures. While most drills are merely practice sessions, there is always the possibility that a real fire or other emergency exists. Study all drill procedures carefully. You will need to proceed calmly and correctly in a real or hypothetical emergency.

• Procedure for releasing students. Children are never allowed to leave the school grounds unless certain requirements are met. Do not rely on a student's word that he is to go home early to keep a dental appointment. Be aware of the circumstances under which a child may be excused in your school district and the paperwork it may involve.

• Attendance record keeping. Attendance is usually taken first thing in the morning. The policy for recording and submitting attendance counts should be made clear. This procedure may include taking a count of those students who are planning to buy lunch or milk that day. If so, how are these to be recorded?

• End of day procedures. Substitutes are expected to leave the classroom in an orderly condition, to turn off lights, lock doors, and close windows. They should leave a note for the returning teacher, along with any collected or corrected papers, and return all keys to the office before leaving for the day. Any other end of day procedure required by the school should be clearly specified.

If any of the above information is not clear to you after reading the manual or handbook, do ask questions at the district office or at the school before beginning to sub.

What symbols are to be used on the roll sheet to note absences, tardies, returning students? Are you responsible for sending this information to the office or is the roll sheet picked up from your room?

Where and how are you to move your class in the event of an emergency drill? What is the correct position to assume under shelter for an air raid or disaster drill?

The more you know before stepping into those first classrooms, the better the job you will do. School personnel agree. For this reason, many districts require teachers to keep an up-to-date Substitute Folder in the classroom or on file in the school office. These folders, if available to you, will probably include the following:

• Class register or seating chart. Once the attendance sheet has left your room in the morning you are often left with nothing to indicate students' names. In taking attendance you will have attempted to memorize two or three names, associating them with student faces. Your ability to call two students by name early in the day will create the impression that you are familiar with the class and are able to identify all the students. You, of course, know that this isn't true. But having a class register or seating chart can be a big help in learning names—and in determining when a child has opted to change seats to be near a friend, as happens with relative frequency!

Some teachers leave notes on these seating charts to indicate who the potential troublemakers or responsible helpers may be.

• Daily or weekly time schedules. These may be of a general nature, indicating which times of the day or week are set aside for each academic subject area, physical education, library study, and so on. It is helpful to know that half the class is excused for choral practice on Tuesday afternoons or that there is an hour-long assembly for all students every Thursday morning. This information will allow you to plan your day around the fixed activities, leaving optional blocks of time for your own projects.

Sometimes these time plan schedules are even more definitive, listing specific chapters or lesson numbers to be studied in each given period.

• Teacher's duty schedule. Since you are expected to fulfill all of the teacher's responsibilities while subbing in his classroom, this list will inform you that Mr. So-and-so has lunch duty on Wednesday or bus duty on Friday afternoon. It will not tell you just exactly what this duty entails. If you are unsure about what you are expected to do, ask at the school office before the duty period arrives.

• Extra information. This may include any information the regular teacher feels will help you to do a more efficient job in the classroom, such as names of helpful neighboring teachers or notes on what the class enjoys doing during free time. It may offer the whereabouts of prepared dittoes or other projects for you to use at your discretion or it may simply encourage you to substitute your own plans or projects as you see fit.

Having a sub folder for handy reference will undoubtedly make your job easier. But what about those classrooms for which no such folder is available? How will you manage to do without what now seems like such vital information?

Much of it can be transmitted to you in one of three common ways.

When you check in at the school office in the morning you may be given, along with your key, an information sheet for the day. It should contain the bell or time schedule, including any unusual circumstances such as early dismissals, planned fire drills, special assemblies, or the like. It will usually make note of your duty assignments or other commitments for the day.

If you are new to the school, the secretary or clerk will show you to the teacher's mailbox where you will pick up any special announcements or bulletins for the class as well as the attendance sheet if it is not already in the classroom. She can also direct you to the teacher's lounge and restrooms and answer any questions you might have.

The second source of information may be a note left for you by the regular teacher. This might give the lesson plan for the day, including applicable texts and chapters, and classroom or homework assignments. Like the sub folder, it may contain notes about special students, suggestions for extra activities, or encouragement to "do your own thing."

On a day when the teacher's note is very sketchy or non-existent, you will know before the students ever arrive that you must rely upon your own knowledge and ingenuity. Granted, it can be a heart-stopping experience for the beginning sub to arrive at the school and find no lesson plan. But this brings us to the third method by which you can gain a sense of security—the data bank stored in your memory.

From all that you have read so far you have gathered, I hope, that a sub must be an observant and resourceful person. Now it is time to put that observation and resourcefulness to the test.

In Chapter 4, I suggested that you spend a day or two visiting in various classrooms. During your visit, you saw the teacher begin the classroom day: pledge of allegiance, attendance, lunch count, and so forth. Now take a deep breath and realize that this is exactly how your own day will begin.

You observed the teacher presenting lessons, supervising activities, moving the class from one area to another. You noted how tests and assignments were corrected, how discipline problems were handled, how the day proceeded in an orderly and constructive fashion.

Even if you have never taught before you have a general idea of what is expected from the teacher and what is expected from the class. All that is missing is an academic program for the day and, if you put on your sleuthing cap, it shouldn't be too difficult to fill in the missing pieces.

Since you have arrived in plenty of time, go to your classroom and have a look at the textbooks on or near the teacher's desk. Most teachers leave reminders for themselves. Chances are the books will be flagged in some way to indicate where the last lesson ended. Make the logical assumption that you may begin precisely where the teacher left off.

In the event that the books are unmarked there are several viable alternatives. Neighboring teachers can be a valuable source of information. Another teacher in the same grade level as the one you are teaching may be able to tell you that this is the week for spelling lesson number fourteen or that Mrs. So-and-so has been working on subjects and predicates.

Collect homework assignments early in the day. The work just completed is a good indication of what is to follow and you may be able to locate correlated chapters in the texts.

Last but far from least, you may check with the students themselves. Children will expect you to be knowledgeable and prepared but they won't expect clairvoyance. Depend on class officers and other responsible children to bring you up to date on what they are presently studying.

Students respond most favorably to subs who appear to be calm and confident. (So, for that matter, do principals and other teachers!) Whether you are dealing with basic procedures or trying to ascertain a lesson plan, ask forthright, pertinent questions and keep your "flustrations" to yourself. Most of all, trust your own good common sense.

Experience, of course, is the best teacher of all. Even a few days in the classroom on your own will make you an "expert" on procedures. So get familiar with as many policies as you can beforehand and *relax* when you get to the classroom.

PART TWO

In the Classroom on Your Own

In Part Two, I want to turn the cameras away from the rudiments of subbing and put the spotlight on you. Now that you know the framework of the job, how do you fit into the picture?

I'll give you four keys for your personal success and take you through the day step by step. By the time we're through you'll feel like a pro. All you need are the keys to your classroom.

8.

Four Keys to Good Subbing

In the preceding chapters we've set the stage for your debut as a sub. Surely you need a good foundation if the job is to be pleasurable and rewarding. But as vital for success as technique may be, there is something else equally important. It is attitude—your approach to the job—the *you* you present to the children.

It is you to whom the children will respond; you as individual as well as teacher. Like puppies on the trail of an interesting new scent, they will pick up your attitudes instantly. The image of yourself you choose to present will make a difference in their acceptance and respect.

I am not suggesting a popularity contest or a bid for friendship on their level. Certainly you must keep a professional distance if you are to maintain your authority. What I am suggesting is attention to demeanor and a look at how successful subs approach their classes.

I have broken this approach into four separate categories and I call them the keys to good subbing. They are simple directives that apply almost anywhere, but they are especially effective for the sub. They are:

1. Be yourself
2. Be positive
3. Be honest
4. Be flexible

Sound simple? Okay. Let's explore them.

BE YOURSELF

If you've ever had a photographer tell you to "smile naturally," you know what happens, don't you? The smile freezes into a forced mask, for who pays attention to how she smiles? Now here I am telling you to "be yourself." What on earth do I mean by that?

I mean take a good look at your own personality and use it to your best advantage. Are you a quiet person? Shy? Do you operate best in peace and quiet? Then your opening words will be slow and soft-spoken. You are making your personality known. "I like quiet voices," you are saying to the students. "We'll get along fine and have some fun, too, if you can be quiet and orderly."

Are you forceful? Dynamic? Used to running the show? It will be there in your voice and in the very way you move about the classroom. "I can tolerate a little noise, some fast pace. But I will be in control at all times."

In each case the students know what to expect. You have projected a pattern for the day, a standard for behavior they can sense. This up-front projection is deceptively simple. It gets across a message about who you are and what it will take to get along with you. Children appreciate this kind of telegraphing.

It would be fruitless to tell you that you will not sometimes be tested to see what your outer limits are. But if you are consistent in your expectations and rewards as well as in your chosen mode of discipline, students will respond to your being yourself by doing as you expect them to.

Don't attempt to be something you are not—a comedian, for example, or a hard-line disciplinarian. Children can sense when you are stepping out of character. It confuses them and tips their sense of balance.

Be as natural in your reactions to them as you would be toward anyone else. If something is funny, by all means, laugh—as long as the joke is not at someone's expense. If you are angered or disappointed in their behavior let them know with a firm, appropriate reminder.

Being yourself implies the freedom to express your personality and interests within the bounds of good judgment. If a lesson about ecology or astronomy strikes a chord in you, expand on it. It will become more meaningful for the students.

I once subbed for three days in a fifth grade classroom when the lead story in the weekly children's newspaper dealt with the bludgeoning of dolphins off the coast of Japan. The children understood the plight of the fishermen whose livelihood was being threatened by the hungry dolphins. At the same time they were incensed by the inhumane manner in which the dolphins were being put to death.

The next day several students brought books and pictures of dolphins. Their discussion had lost none of its fervor. Since I am a great believer in letters and it seemed important to the children, I suggested we write letters to our government indicating our concern. This presented a great opportunity for a lesson in the correct form of the letter as well as a forum for expressing their feelings.

Weeks later, the regular teacher told me the class was thrilled to have received a signed letter from the president informing them that their inquiry had been routed for study to the Department of the Interior.

Another time I subbed in a sixth grade classroom on a day when the children were scheduled for scoliosis screening. (Scoliosis is a curvature of the spine which must be detected and treated early in order to prevent disfigurement.) The students were noticeably nervous and skeptical, not to mention embarrassed at having to be examined by the school nurse. One or two had been singled out for further testing, and anxiety was running high.

I happen to have a severe curvature myself, although it is not easily seen when I am clothed. I am well acquainted with the simple methods for detection and with the means of treatment. I am a living example that it is perfectly possible to lead a normal life even though one has such a curvature.

I could have kept my mouth shut and simply gone on to other things. But I felt the children might benefit from my experience and reassurance. I allowed a few students to trace the path of my spine and spoke with them candidly about the curvature I've had since I was twelve. Sure enough, their relief was tangible as their understanding grew. Soon we were able to move on to the day's activities in a relaxed and normal way.

I mention these incidents simply to point out that I choose to relate to my students with the whole of me, not just the part that is capable of teaching fractions. Children appreciate this sharing of yourself. If I have been successful as a sub, this is certainly one of the reasons for it.

Children frequently want to know if you are married and if you have children. They ask about your hobbies and your travels. This is not meant to be an invasion of your privacy. It is natural and simple curiosity. Feel free to reveal as much of this personal side of yourself as you wish—no more—and only when doing so serves the worthwhile purpose of opening lines of communication.

Do take care *not* to make the classroom your soapbox. This is not the place to advocate political, religious, or personal convictions that are outside the sphere of classroom interest. It is one thing to give of yourself and your experience, quite another to inflict your views on others.

Perhaps in saying, "Be yourself," I am really saying, "Be your best self"; your natural, well-mannered, sensitive, and most discriminating self.

BE POSITIVE

For many reasons, especially as a beginning sub, a positive attitude is the most precious commodity you can carry into the classroom.

If that sounds exaggerated, think again. It is your attitude that will set the tone for the day, your outlook and expectations to which children respond. If you are sure and confident, friendly and interested, the class is likely to be the same. Taking their cue from you, they will proceed on a steady course, not too dissimilar from the one they take under the guidance of their regular teacher. It is a well-charted course, familiar and, perforce, not to be tampered with.

If, on the other hand, you are tense, uncertain, grouchy, or just plain bored, be assured you will transmit this to your class. Children being what they are, they will pounce upon the opportunity to match you grouch for grouch and to find new and ingenious ways to try your patience and endurance.

You will smile, therefore, even though your feet hurt and your Great Aunt Tess is coming for dinner. You will keep a friendly, upbeat pace because it is in your own best interest, as well as the students', to do so.

Well, you may say, every teacher is entitled to an off day. Perhaps so. But *you* are a sub. You are not dealing with the daily pressures and problems of the regular teacher. You accepted this assignment though you knew your Great Aunt Tess was coming to dinner, and now that you are here you will put forth your best and expect the best from your students.

I have seen a class disintegrate before my very eyes because I became preoccupied or testy. Letting go of the reins causes a well-known syndrome of deteriorating behavior every experienced sub will recognize. I bestow upon you the benefit of my experience. Children will sense that you are not as alert as you should be and will, out of their own boredom, begin to try all sorts of fun and games.

Sometimes the material you are covering is repetitious or dull, or the children have just been sitting there too long. Whatever the reason for their restless inattention you must instigate a positive change of pace.

Pull some Brainteasers or other wonderful fare from your well-stocked bag of tricks (see Part Three) and seize the spontaneous and happy reactions to get yourself back on course.

Granted, this spirit-lifting interlude may play havoc with the scheduled lesson plan. But it will serve a far greater purpose in restoring interest and attentiveness so that you can return to the lessons at hand. And since the activities you choose are educational in their own right, you have merely traded one area of learning for another while fulfilling your primary obligation as a sub—maintaining order and progress in the absence of the regular teacher.

Your positive attitude must extend to every area from discipline to recreation to the presentation of ideas. Like a tour guide who travels the same route day after day, you will strive for freshness and enthusiasm in order to keep your group interested and eager.

BE HONEST

As a child I was maddeningly inquisitive. Accustomed to taking long walks with my father, I could come up with endless questions about everything from airplanes to zebras. More often than not my poor father could not answer with certainty. What he did do was foster a lasting friendship between me and books.

Together, we would traverse the dictionary, the atlas, the encyclopedia until the elusive answers appeared. Happily absorbed in this pursuit, I never thought to doubt the scope of my father's knowledge or, in fact, to care. He made a game of finding the answers and it was a game I enjoyed.

As a sub I use much the same sort of honesty with my classes, and get much the same response. I do not know all there is to know about waterways and I don't pretend to know. But if the lesson at hand is foreign to me, I know how to make an enjoyable game of seeking information. I may assign "teams" or we may work as a class, using the school library or resources in the room.

The learning is meaningful because the children have been involved in the process. My lack of knowledge has become an asset rather than a disadvantage.

If the lesson involves mathematical concepts (not my long suit!) I may ask a student who understands the solution to explain it to the rest of us. Children love to play teacher and I have discovered that there is a mathematical whiz in nearly every classroom. If there is not, and the material seems increasingly confusing, I'll suggest that we drop that lesson for today and leave it for their more experienced teacher.

Students in the elementary school setting can and do accept a sub's occasional lack of knowledge if the lapse is presented honestly and appropriately. Bluffing, on the other hand, or refusing to admit one's mistake, is understandably asking for trouble.

The same kind of honesty is called for with regard to procedures. You have done your best to become . acquainted with school rules and regulations. But if you don't know how to run this blankety-blank film projector, admit it! You have a choice of abandoning the scheduled film or getting help from someone who does.

It is more important to get the job done than to worry about your injured self-esteem. Interestingly, you will have an easier time by enlisting the help and support of your students than by pretending to know more than you do.

BE FLEXIBLE

If there is a watchword for your career in subbing, flexibility must certainly be that word. At every turn you are faced with options and decisions about lesson planning, discipline, and procedure.

Every school, every class, every day is different and must be approached with that in mind. You must learn to assess the advantages and disadvantages of each situation and deal with it in the most effective way.

Picture yourself in these typical situations and the meaning of flexibility becomes clear:

The teacher has left you a detailed lesson plan with every hour preplanned. But it is the day before a four-day holiday and the class is as high as a kite. Do you struggle doggedly to complete each task or do you opt for a more relaxed day by substituting some other activities?

The class has returned from a worthwhile assembly on a subject that really sparked their interest. Do you forge right ahead with the scheduled spelling test or delay it half an hour, making time for discussion or debate?

The sun is shining after four days of rain and the children look longingly at the playground. There's no chance to run because the fields are too muddy. Do you stick to the study period scheduled for after lunch or lead a ten-minute indoor relay to work off pent-up energies before getting back to work?

In each case your assessment of the situation has led you to juggle the schedule. Of course there is work to be done and much to be accomplished. But being alert to the interest and temperament of your class and adjusting routines accordingly will make for a more fruitful day.

On days when you are working from a skimpy lesson plan, flexibility is even more important. Matching your skills and interests with those of your class, you may decide to make an interesting foray into the world of science, let's say, or drama.

You may choose to conduct experiments from materials at hand or to make posters on the theme of ecology. You may have the class read a play aloud or have small groups produce their own short skits. By choosing activities within your own expertise you are enriching the curriculum of this particular class in a unique and desirable way.

Being flexible does not mean looking for ways to veer off the established course. It does mean weighing the options you have as a sub to fulfill your duties in the most productive and meaningful manner.

Flexibility counts when it comes to discipline, as well. Every class, reflecting the values of the regular teacher, has its own milieu, its own pace. What is viewed as high-spirited enthusiasm by one teacher may be seen as outright bedlam by another. You will need to judge for yourself what seems to be acceptable behavior for *this particular* class. The children themselves will tip you off by their own conditioned reflexes as to whether this class is expected to seek permission to leave their seats or is allowed free access to the pencil sharpener and the restroom by just getting up at will.

Don't be too hasty to pounce on questionable behavior. Allow for an hour of "settling in" until you make that all-important judgment. Then, using your own expectations as a guideline, make the most consistent decisions you can so that things don't get out of control.

I have subbed in classrooms where freedom of movement was considered a boon to productivity, and in others where getting up for a drink of water without permission was viewed as a serious breach. With as much flexibility as I am able to muster, I try to carry on in the footsteps of the regular teacher while maintaining my own sense of what feels right.

So there you have them—four keys to unlock the mystery of what makes a really good sub. To be happy and successful in this career you need to put forth your very best self. Regardless of your knowledge, your experience or your inexperience, your attitude can make the difference.

9.

___

On a Typical Day

On a typical day your phone will ring sometime around six A.M. "Good morning." The sub clerk is wide awake. "This is the Sub Center. Can you work today?"

You are tempted for a moment to go right back to sleep, but your better nature—and a fleeting premonition about next month's heating bill—soon rouse you to attention. "Yes," you murmur. "What have we got today?"

"I have a second grade at Maplegrove and a sixth grade at Walnut. Any preference?"

You deliberate briefly, weighing the quiet, expectant second graders against the rowdy challenge of the sixth. No doubt the little ones would make for an easier day. But the older kids can be a lot of fun, you are familiar with Walnut School, and besides, it's almost Christmas and there's a new art project you've been wanting to try. "I'll take the sixth," you say.

"Good. Eight o'clock to two forty-five. Mrs. Brown's class. Have a nice day."

As you fling back the covers, your mind races to meet the day. You had hoped to take Grandma to lunch this afternoon and to get some shopping done. The trouble with subbing is that you rarely know beforehand which days you will be teaching. Well, those plans will wait. Now, where'd I put those instructions for paper sculpture?

Half an hour before the start of the class you check in at the school office. "Good morning," the secretary greets you. "Are you Mrs. Brown today?"

You smile at the familiar question, proud of your ability to wear a succession of new hats. You accept the key and scan the daily schedule. You have playground duty at morning recess. There's a citizenship assembly at 9:30. That may mean rearranging your lesson plan.

Picking up the roll sheet, you check Mrs. Brown's mail box for announcements or notices, and then head for the teachers' lounge. Many staff faces are familiar. You are greeted with "Good morning," and "Who are you today?" You introduce yourself to those who don't know you and put your brown bag in the refrigerator.

You might have opted to buy a school lunch today or to leave campus at lunch hour for a quick run to the bank and a local drive-in hamburger stand. As it is, you packed your own diet special and you now have time for a cup of coffee before going to your room.

In the classroom, ten minutes before the bell, you read the teacher's note and check the plan book. "Dear Sub," Mrs. Brown has written, "please review chapter 14 in math book and have children do problems 1–20 on page 196.

"Give spelling test for lesson 16 in spelling book and assign lesson 17 for class or homework. They can do social studies maps or library reading and a composition on Christmas Vacation or any other project you want to use. They are a little wild—it's so close to vacation—so use your own judgment. Thanks, and have a nice day."

Like many lesson plans this one is simple and flexible. You decide to work on math from 8:00 to 8:45, while class concentration is greatest. You can get the spelling test out of the way, and corrected, before the morning assembly. After recess they can work on spelling lesson 17 in class to avoid the need for homework. That will leave the afternoon free for reading or composition and for the art project you want to try.

By the time the class is seated you have located the proper textbooks and checked the layout of the room. You are smiling and organized, ready to begin your day. You can sense that the kids are indeed full of holiday excitement. You will need to be cheerful but firm.

On a typical day in the K–6 grades, you will try to memorize a few student names quickly, perhaps by associating three names on the attendance sheet with the redhead in the corner, the tall boy in the rear, and the little blonde with glasses in the front row.

You will call on these three by name, early in the morning, for one reason or another. Doing so will give both you and the class some measure of confidence. "If you know our names," they will reason silently, "then you have some control over our destiny. You are actively the teacher—at least for today."

As you call the roll and make the opening announcements, preparing to present the first lesson, you will begin to size up today's class. Are they alert and organized? Are they attentive or wisecracking? You can learn a lot in the first twenty minutes of the day that will help you to choose supplementary activities suited to their level and temperament.

Just as the teacher, upon returning to the class, can tell a lot about the effectiveness of the sub, so can the sub, by the initial response of the class, judge a lot about the effectiveness of the teacher. Generally, early in the day a class responds much as it might for the regular teacher—at least until it has the chance to size *you* up. Are you confident and friendly? Do you seem to know what you are doing? Are you likely to brook a lot of nonsense?

Obviously then, it is important to put your best foot forward quickly. Chapter 10 will tell you how to manage those first vital moments with aplomb. For now, take careful note of the reasons why you must set the stage early for a productive and successful day.

On a typical day you will present new material, such as this math lesson, slowly and with appropriate emphasis. Use the blackboard to illustrate. Have the children participate. Interpret instructions as you go. Ask questions. Do they seem to understand?

Watch their faces. Do they seem perplexed? Be prepared to repeat and repeat. Give different examples. Question them again. Does the process—the idea—now seem clear?

It is important to establish two-way communication. That's the only way you'll know what they have learned. Lecturing has no place in the K–6 classroom. Children often hear but do not listen. Ask questions. Repeat instructions if you must. Attack the problem from a new angle if you can, trying to zero in on the root of their confusion, and clarifying with patience and simplicity.

On the other hand, don't belabor the point. There is a fine line between comprehension and boredom and it's a line you don't want to cross. Watch for the light of dawn to break. Then pack your bags and move on.

One of the difficulties every teacher encounters is the varying length of time from dawn to daylight. There are always those who catch on quickly and finish problem 10 while others still stare miserably at number one. Teachers develop their own ways for dealing with this. For the sub, here's a suggestion or two.

When you are explaining a concept to the entire class, stick with it until most seem to have it. There will be other opportunities for the slower learners to catch on. You may find time, during quiet work, for individual conferences as needed. Otherwise, in your note to the teacher at the end of the day, point out that several students need extra help. Mention them by name if you can.

Chances are, they are the same slower children the teacher regularly deals with and it will come as no news or surprise. Don't risk losing the rest of the class to boredom for the benefit of a few. Boredom and inactivity lead to disaster. Avoid them if you want to keep control.

In a situation where the students are working independently on a paper or project, again there will be those who finish early. To discourage inactivity, you may wish to suggest several alternatives:

1. Tell students who finish with time to spare that they may read for pleasure or use the time to catch up on homework or project preparation.

2. Distribute a piece of drawing paper to each student early in the day. Those who complete the work before the rest of the class are free to draw quietly while waiting.

3. Keep available a small stack of books, magazines, and puzzles that efficient students may choose from your desk while waiting for the group to finish.

4. Become familiar enough with the Bag of Tricks in Part Three to select appropriate and quiet timefillers for the early birds. Take care not to choose timefillers that may be distracting to the other students or that are so attractive that sloppy work is traded for their allure. Your purpose is to keep students busy at all times, not to lure them away from their primary occupation with learning.

On a typical day you will establish the rules for classroom behavior early and be consistent in your application of them. Often, rules are posted in the classroom. If not, you may be sure the children are well acquainted with the limits of acceptable behavior.

Specific disciplinary techniques are discussed in Chapter 10. What is important here is that you remember the need for being consistent about what you expect and the disciplinary actions you take. No one is quicker than a child to point out the inequities of life! "But he did it and you didn't say anything!" is a sure way of losing control.

Into every substitute's life can come that sinking feeling of losing control. No matter how firm, friendly, consistent, and wonderful you have been, the little darlings simply don't appreciate you.

Perhaps they are bored. Tired. Overexcited. Maybe they just don't like subs. Whatever the reason, the noise level increases, there is shuffling about and a general deafness to the pearls that are spilling from your lips.

Sometimes, when this happens, there is a great temptation to spin your wheels and let the day slide to its inevitable conclusion. But on a typical day you will remember to maintain your positive outlook. You *can* get back into the driver's seat. What is needed is a shift of gears: Get their attention and move on.

Once you have achieved a moment of silence by flicking the light switch or ringing a small bell, use your quietest voice to remind them, without sarcasm, that this is a classroom.

Don't lecture and don't threaten, unless you are prepared to follow through by sending offenders to the office or restricting playground time. Give them a minute to wrap up the current project. Then shift quickly to the next.

Children who have been working quietly on a succession of academic materials sometimes simply need a break. That is one reason for recess. But even an hour and a half or two hours of steady concentration can be too much when you're ten years old.

Suggest a stretch, or even a jog around their desks. Allow for a moment of noisy groaning. But at a given signal they are to return to their seats and be ready for what's coming next.

"What's coming next," of course, is entirely up to you. Choose a ten-minute timefiller for them to have fun with before you return to the schedule. Or return right away with an intriguing promise that there's a fun period coming up if they can get the work done quickly and quietly.

Use this as a simple method of positive reinforcement. Working well is rewarded. Remember that you do not have the regular teacher's built-in authority or his familiar routines to fall back on. You must therefore devise your own methods for keeping control, and I have found that this is one of the best. Certainly it is far more effective and a lot easier on your nerves than anger or sarcasm or threat.

Children returning from lunch period recess are often excited and tired. On a typical day you may borrow a favorite ploy of many teachers by choosing that time to read a story. Regular teachers often read a chapter a day from a really exciting children's novel. Since your time is limited, try a picture book or a classic short story, depending upon the grade level.

Use this storytime as a springboard to a craft or drama project if time allows, or simply as a welcome quiet time before getting back to business.

In choosing and using fun periods wisely you are overcoming the greatest obstacle to substitute success: failure to get and keep the attention of the class in a positive and constructive way.

On a typical day you will correct all papers insofar as it is possible to do so. Direct students to exchange papers with a neighbor, going over the answers together. Have them put the number of wrong answers in a circle at the top of the page, return papers to their owners for quick reference, and turn them in to you for their teacher.

If the answers are subjective or otherwise difficult to evaluate, then merely collect the papers. Corrected or not, stack them on the teacher's desk with an explanatory note whenever necessary. Do not assign letter grades to the papers or enter grades in the gradebook. That is the teacher's domain.

Use classroom supplies carefully and sparingly, being sure that scissors and crayons are returned to the shelves by the end of the day. Have students distribute supplies so that control is maintained; don't invite children to help themselves. School budgets, like family budgets, are tight these days and do not allow for waste or "mysterious disappearance." Extra supplies are usually available in the office or storeroom if you need them.

A teacher recently related to me her sad tale of the broken crayons. It seems that after weeks of bits and nubbins, a new stock of crayons finally arrived—on the day before her necessary absence. When she returned she found the new crayons in pieces—broken, the kids said, at the request of the sub whose art project required broken crayons! Whether the sub had, in fact, requested this is a matter of speculation. More likely, the kids had found it a happy little pastime while the sub's attention was elsewhere. In either case the results were the same—an unhappy teacher back where she started from and a sub not likely to return.

Keeping your eyes open and your head on your shoulders is a big part of being a sub. All the knowledge and enthusiasm in the world won't make up for a lack of common sense.

By the end of this typical day you have dealt with lost lunch money and forgotten homework. You've conquered playground rushes, student crushes, leaky noses, tissue roses, and a host of other problems, big and small. And you've come to the sane and inescapable conclusion that there's no such thing as a typical day at all.

For the sub each day is a new adventure, each classroom a whole new world. Still, you have begun to see yourself in the picture. Now, let's sharpen up the focus.

10.

Your Day from Start to Finish (K–6)

GETTING STARTED

In every classroom there is a ripple of excitement when you—the sub—walk through the door instead of dear old well-known Mrs. So-and-so. You will sense it in the babble of voices—a mixture of apprehension, nervousness, giddiness—the moment you enter the room.

Children are creatures of habit. They know their classroom routine and their teacher's personality as well as they know their own names. Your presence is at once a threat and a challenge. Who are you? Will you like them? What will their day be like?

Even in classrooms where there are teacher's aides who know the children and the daily schedule, make no mistake about it. It is you who will set the tone for the day, and you will do it in the very first few minutes.

Take a positive attitude, a firm step, and a big smile with you as you stride to the head of the class. Your cheery "Good morning!" will likely be met with a raucous chorus of "good mornings" in return. But your sunny attitude and your clear implication that this *will* be a good morning will not be missed by these thirty pairs of watchful, waiting eyes.

As you begin to hear questions— "Where's Mrs. So-and-so?" and "Are you a sub?"—and a general shuffling of feet and books, turn your back to the class and write your name, very clearly, and today's date on the blackboard. There is an old teaching adage, use your chalk, not your voice, when you want to achieve quiet in the classroom.

Turning back to the class, you may now introduce yourself in a calm and pleasant manner. "I'm Mrs. Jones. I'm sorry your teacher can't be with you today, but I'm happy to be here in her place. We're going to have a day much like your days when she is here. And we'll try to have some fun along the way."

At this point you will want to call the roll, as most school districts need attendance counts early. Remember that children are sensitive about their names. If you see a name that stymies you, ask for help. You may read the surname first or read the given name and ask for pronunciation of the surname. You will gain a friend in Johnny Mekalopoulos if you ask for help with his name rather than mangle it in front of his laughing friends. If you do make a mistake, apologize and move on.

When taking the roll in a K–6 class you may wish to ask the children to let you know, as they respond, if they have a particular job in the classroom such as president, paper monitor, or the like. Make a mental note of some of these. Generally, these are responsible students who can be depended upon throughout the day for various needs or errands.

In some upper grade classrooms, there may be a roll monitor who does this job for the teacher. Let him proceed as usual if you like. But if you prefer to call the roll yourself so that you can begin to become familiar with the students' names, then do so.

A good rule of thumb, in calling the roll or any other procedure, is: Try to do things as closely as possible to the way the regular teacher does them. But what works for a teacher who knows her students may not feel right for you. If it becomes a question of your personal comfort, feel free to do things your way.

Many schools require a count of those children who are buying lunch or milk each day. If this is true in your school, take the count right after roll call.

If there is a flag salute monitor, let him or her lead the salute. If not, lead it yourself, saying, "Please rise . . . ready . . . begin."

GREAT EXPECTATIONS

Now the day has begun in earnest and all eyes are turned toward you. It is impossible to overemphasize how important it is to maintain a positive outlook. Generally, we get what we expect.

There is a legend in one school district about the sub who marched to the front of the class without ever removing her coat. She wrote assignment after assignment on the blackboard and sat perched on the edge of the desk, glowering all day at the children. Her attitude dared them to try anything funny. She expected the worst—and she got it. There are always a few children who will take the dare gladly and it wasn't long before notes went sailing through the air, loud noises prevailed, and shenanigans triumphed, though her angry glares met a sea of innocent faces. Her classrooms were a shambles but the word spread quickly and very soon she was "spared" the chore of subbing.

While Mrs. Glower's attitude was, of course, extreme, it does point up what we are saying. A firm but *friendly* attitude from a sub who expects the best will bring out the best in her students.

How does one establish this ideal atmosphere in which

the sub and the students will flourish? The answers are as varied as the subs. Specific suggestions for using your own personality and interests are discussed in Chapter 8 and Part Three.

For now, we will concentrate on some general guidelines to maintaining a classroom conducive to learning.

The most obvious way to establish your expectations is to tell the class what you expect. Both you and the students are aware that there are certain classroom rules that they are expected to obey; things like courtesy, raising hands before speaking, etc. Beyond that, it is up to you to stress what is important to you.

If you insist on a quiet classroom—and this is a reasonable expectation—make that clear. Tell the students you do not plan to speak above their voices. Establish a signal, the ringing of a small bell, perhaps, or the flicking of a light switch. When the signal is given it means the noise level is too high and you want quiet.

Reminding the children that you expect them to abide by their regular teacher's rules, keep your own rules simple and brief. A long list of do's and don't's will not only be forgotten, but will overburden short attention spans.

Now you have established your attitude, completed the opening procedures, and set forth your rules, all in the first few minutes. On to the fun part. What may the students expect of you?

For one thing, keep a Superstars list on the blackboard. On one side of the board write "Superstars" (or "Good Guys," or "I Am the Greatest," or any other positive title that strikes you). Explain that you will be looking, all day, for people to add to that list; people who work quietly and efficiently, who contribute to the class, who are helpful and courteous and nice to be around. Tell the students that the list will remain on the board for their teacher to see the next day.

This simple tool of positive reinforcement is one to which

children respond. You may wish to reward your Superstars with leading the lunch line, early recess, fifteen minutes of free time during the day or any other school-approved treat. For many, being on the list is its own reward. It is amazing how hard even the older students will try—and ask you to observe them—to make it to the list.

Children who continue to do outstanding work may be rewarded with check marks or asterisks next to their names. A name may also be removed from the list as a result of poor behavior, but the child should have the chance to be reinstated if behavior improves for the rest of the day.

A variation of this method is to write "We are Superstars today" on the board and have the class come up one at a time so each child can write his name. (If you have a fair memory, this in addition to roll call can give you a good start toward learning children's names.)

In using this variation, a child who misbehaves is asked to come up and erase his own name. Meting out his own punishment in this way often spurs a resolve to improve so that he may add his name by the end of the day.

We caution you not to add or delete names from your list more than once. The idea behind this positive reward system is that one infraction need not be held against a child all day. But its greatest value is in simply recognizing good work.

Most fun of all is a second list you may keep on the board, this one labeled Brainteaser Champs. Brainteasers are simple word puzzles, math progressions, or tests of logic that can quickly be written on the board to be "solved," just as quickly, by the students. (Dozens of samples from which to choose are given in Chapter 13.)

Used as a reward when the class is working well, brainteasers are an effective tool for keeping order and interest in the classroom day. Students should be told that at any time during the day you may say, "Look up. Here comes a brainteaser!" and you will write one on the board.

As the names of the puzzle solvers are added to the Brainteaser Champs list, this provides you with another way in which to recognize students.

The children should be told that an entire row or table may be disqualified from the next brainteaser for poor behavior, or that they will stop completely if the class as a whole is unruly. Since students in all grade levels love this spontaneous break from routine as well as the challenge of solving the puzzles, the Brainteaser Champs list is a wonderful method for maintaining order in the classroom.

ABOUT DISCIPLINE

We have been discussing positive attitudes and reinforcement techniques that have proven to be helpful aids for the successful substitute teacher. Ideally, the use of these aids in addition to your cheerful expectations and your academic preparedness will result in a happy and productive day.

In reality, of course, the sub must be prepared to handle an infinite variety of discipline problems in the course of a given day.

Hyperactive youngsters and children with learning disabilities or educational handicaps can present special problems with restlessness or general unruliness. In many schools these children are removed from the regular classroom for part of the day for participation in special classes. For the time that they are in your room, dealing with them requires patience, tact, and a firm guiding hand. There are good reading resources available for learning about dealing with children with special problems. Here we will confine ourselves to handling the everyday problems that occur, from time to time, in every room.

Like children left in the care of a new sitter, students will frequently set out to test the patience, knowledge, and resources of the unknown substitute teacher. Often the very same youngsters who try the patience of the regular teacher, they will simply attempt to take advantage of your inexperience in their class.

Switching seats to be near a friend, telling you "the way Mrs. So-and-so does it," chewing gum, or chattering constantly are commonplace situations that can be disruptive to the class. Annoying or hitting other students is an even more serious offense. Since many of these infractions are known to be forbidden, you may simply need to remind the class that you are as aware of the rules as they in order to restore order.

As for "the way Mrs. So-and-so does it," we remind you that you are in charge here. Your intention is, as we have said, to keep things as close to the normal routine as possible in order to minimize disruption. But when you are offered conflicting "helpful" advice, or when you simply do not feel comfortable with "the way Mrs. So-and-so does it," feel free to set your own rules for bathroom visits, test correction, moving from class to playground, or any other procedures with which you must deal.

Remember that the keys to successful subbing are a positive attitude, honesty, and flexibility. Flexibility means not only adapting to different classroom routines daily, but helping students adjust to new ways of doing things as well. Mutual respect for each other's needs, opinions, and feelings is essential in our daily lives. Successful give-and-take within the classroom framework provides a valuable lesson to students. Listen to reason. Then make decisions firmly, to the best of your ability, and stick to them.

Behaving decisively is the surest way to maintain a position of authority. When you are faced with a child or a group of children who repeatedly act out, you must deal with them firmly or face the prospect of losing control.

Changing a child's seat or moving him to a remote part

of the room may be all that is necessary to change his attitude.

Also, you may wish to start a third list on the blackboard. This one can be called "Sour Apples" or "In Trouble Today" or any other title that implies discipline problems. Often, seeing one's name go on that list is enough to prompt better behavior. Having the offender write his own name on the list can be even more effective.

Here, again, a child should be given the opportunity to remove his name from the list if his subsequent actions improve. However, if he continues to be disruptive you must be ready to take sterner measures.

From your pre-subbing orientation (see Chapter 1) you are familiar with your district's policy regarding detention. By all means, make the child a candidate for detention if he warrants it.

Keep your anger under control. Do not take the child's acting out as a personal affront or as a threat to your effectiveness. Use your chalk instead of your voice (that is, the Sour Apples or Detention List if used in your district) whenever possible.

But if you are faced with a student who refuses to conform or who poses a physical or emotional threat to you or the class, *do not hesitate to ask for assistance.* If there is a telephone in the room, use it to call the office. If not, send a monitor with a note requesting help. Never strike a child, or assume you are reasoning with a rational youngster who, in fact, may have emotional problems of which you are not aware. Ask to have the child removed from your room either temporarily or for the rest of the day.

In most cases, the need for this last resort is rare. But a feeling that you are in control is vital to your success as a sub and there are no medals for bravery in dealing with repeated offenders. Do not risk danger or extreme aggravation to yourself or to your class. If you need help, get it.

THE ACADEMIC DAY

It is not accidental that we leave a discussion of the academic day to the end of this chapter. For many subs (even those of you with an abysmal fear of fractions), guiding the class through the academic day will be the easiest part of your assignment.

In most classrooms the absent teacher will have left a lesson plan of some sort for your use. Some plans are very complete, listing textbooks, chapters, and worksheets to be used as well as a timetable for each subject area, recess, and lunch break. Others may be only general guidelines indicating the type of work to be done at various times of the day. Some lesson plans may even suggest alternative ideas to be used at your discretion.

The most important thing for you as a sub to remember about a lesson plan is that it is not a bible.

As a qualified sub, you are expected to be reasonably competent in most subject areas. Particularly in the K–6 grades, it is likely you will be familiar with the subject matter, though some of the methods for teaching may have changed since you made your acquaintance with them.

In many schools teachers are provided with "Teaching Editions" of each textbook. These contain answers to all problems as well as instruction in teaching the lesson. Of course they make it infinitely easier to answer students' questions reliably and accurately.

But whether or not you are provided with these instructional aids, learn to rely on your own proficiency as you go along.

Remember that one of the keys to good subbing is honesty. You are not expected to be Mr. or Mrs. Perfect and there is no crime in not knowing the answer.

Together, you and your students can consult reference material and textbooks. Use the school library. Assign task groups. Turn your lack of knowledge about amphibians and reptiles into a lesson no one will soon forget.

And now a word for those of you with that incurable fear of fractions (or adverbs, or times tables, or commas). Again we remind you that the lesson plan is not a bible.

If you would rather parse a Shakespearean sonnet, would rather, in fact, face a cageful of lions, than teach a lesson in common denominators, then for heaven's sake—don't teach it!

Neither the district's national standing nor the students' eventual college prep scores will suffer irreparably if you do not teach common denominators on any given day.

Feel perfectly free to change the lesson plan or to shift its emphasis to areas in which you feel most comfortable. Chart your own course, use your own skills, draw freely from your own bag of tricks (See Chapter 12) to make the day both productive and gratifying. Be flexible in your schedule to allow for such unforeseen events as assemblies, band practice, or thunderstorms. Like the Boy Scouts, the substitute must always be prepared.

ALL'S WELL THAT ENDS WELL

Toward the end of the day, leave time for students to clean up before leaving. Remind monitors to do such chores as closing windows, emptying trash cans, and the like. Your capability as a sub will, in part, be judged by whether or not you leave a room as neat as when you entered.

Remind your students about homework assignments. Notices going home stand a better chance of getting home if you distribute them now, at the end of the day.

Compliment those who made the Superstars and Brainteaser Champs lists. Tell all the students you enjoyed the class if, indeed, you did and wish them all a pleasant afternoon.

It is standard procedure to leave a note for the returning teacher. Tell him what academic work was accomplished and in which areas you feel students need help or review.

Make him aware of any unusual problems or noteworthy deeds that occurred during the day.

Explain simply the basis for your Superstars and Brainteaser Champs lists and ask that he personally commend those students for their good work.

Take a final look around the room to be sure that doors are locked, windows closed, and lights off. Turn in your key, thank the office staff for any help they may have provided, and smile! You've done a good day's work and there's still half a day in which to follow other pursuits.

And be assured, good news travels fast. If you've done a good job you'll be called to work again. And again and again and again.

11.

The Junior and Senior High School Day

The mechanics of the junior high and high school differ considerably from those of the elementary school. Since your role as a sub is necessarily different as well, a special chapter dealing with them is included here to help you see yourself at the head of these classrooms.

At this level, of course, you will no longer be concerned with leaky noses and tissue paper roses. Students at this stage are expected to work somewhat independently and to take on some of the responsibility of dawning adulthood, although some adjust more easily than others.

Seventh and eighth graders, especially, are undergoing that great transition I spoke of earlier and sometimes require an extra measure of understanding as well as a firm push forward. Teachers and subs who work with these youngsters have the dubious distinction, but often the very real reward, of watching the metamorphosis take place.

The four keys to good subbing—being yourself, being positive, being honest and flexible—most assuredly apply here. You will want to relate to your classes in a candid, forthright, and natural manner. These twelve to eighteen year olds are quick to spot a phony and are far more adept than their younger counterparts at turning your lack of confidence and authority to their advantage.

You will want to be thoroughly familiar with school rules and procedures, from readmitting an absent or tardy student to following a fluctuating bell schedule. Most school offices provide such information in the sub folder. Read it thoroughly before reporting to your first class.

It helps to have a working knowledge of the subject you are covering, although I have known art majors who subbed in science classes and managed very well. Often at this level, the regular teacher leaves a study assignment for his classes that the sub is expected to supervise but not actively teach. Most teachers leave such independent work not because they doubt your ability to teach but because they know there is a likelihood you may be subbing in an unfamiliar area. Still, there is an obvious advantage in being able to answer questions with some degree of expertise.

In the junior high setting you may wish to state a preference, then, for subbing in the areas of your greatest strength. At the high school level some states require certification in specific subject areas, although your willingness to accept other assignments in a pinch can make you a valuable asset to the district.

In fact, the primary differences between subbing in the K–6 grades and in the high school are the limited scope of the subject matter you take on and the shorter length of time spent with each class. Because of these differences the need for brainteasers and other spontaneous timefillers diminishes greatly, as does the personal relationship you build with each class.

These older students, upon completing the day's assignment, should no longer need incentives or busy work. They are more reasonably directed to read for another class or to get a head start on homework. Generally, they appreciate this unexpected "catch-up" time and are more than willing to use it wisely.

When reporting for duty in the junior high or high school, check in early enough to become familiar with the day's schedule and with the assignment left by the teacher for each class. Learn the location of the teachers' lounge and restrooms, if this is an unfamiliar school, as well as the location of the department office for the subject you are covering. The department head can be a great help in suggesting supplementary work if the teacher has left no assignment and, in schools this large, it helps to know your way around before you begin.

Introduce yourself to your first class, stating that you will be covering all of Mr. Blank's classes for today. Write your name on the blackboard with today's date.

Call the roll, noting absences and tardies. In many schools students returning from an absence must bring a readmittance card to be signed by each teacher. The card, issued by the attendance office, indicates that the absence was excused and discourages the cutting of classes. Follow the procedure in your district for keeping accurate records. Usually, the attendance card for each period is picked up by an office monitor sometime during each hour.

Read aloud any announcements pertaining to the class regarding schedule changes or special events. Then, if there is a study or written assignment for the period, write it on the blackboard, spelling out instructions clearly. Let the students know whether it is to be collected before the end of the hour or may be completed at home. Answer any questions about materials or instructions and expect the class to work quietly and independently for the rest of the session.

You may be asked to show a film or play a record or tape as part of the daily assignment. Time at the end of the hour may be used to discuss this audiovisual presentation or to have the students complete a written evaluation.

In cases where no assignment has been left or it is insufficient for the allotted time, feel free to lead a class discussion on a related subject or to direct the students to work on required material for this or any other class.

Regardless of the particular assignment, you are justified in expecting students to work responsibly and with initiative. Remember that, whether seventh graders or eleventh, junior high and high school students are treated as maturing adults, with appropriate behavior anticipated.

Allow for the occasional "accidentally" dropped book, the heaved sigh, or other brief laugh-provoking interruption. Expect a whispered exchange or two or the passing of a ruler or pencil. Kids are human and an hour of quiet concentration is not their favorite occupation. In the absence of a regular give-and-take class time they are apt to become fidgety or bored.

What you are striving for, in your role as a sub, is an atmosphere both relaxed and conducive to learning. You are neither a warden nor a Casper Milquetoast and you must expect reasonable quiet and attention. If students are unruly, remind them that others are trying to work and that their cooperation is necessary. Anyone who persists in creating a disturbance can be sent to the office at your request.

Generally, students are aware of this option and will stay within reasonable limits. While some hours may somehow seem longer than others, soon you will face a new group.

While the class is working, prepare any materials or instructions you may need for the incoming group. Announce when five minutes of work time remains and allow enough time for collection of papers. When the bell sounds you will have about five minutes until the new class assembles.

Roll call and announcements will be repeated for each class as the day moves ahead. Keep notes regarding progress or problems experienced with each hour so that you can report them accurately to the returning teacher.

During recess breaks, lunch hour, or any free periods in the teacher's schedule, you may relax in the faculty lounge or dining room. Check with the office to see whether you are expected to be available for the teacher's conference periods, and always lock the door when leaving the room.

At the end of the day leave a note for the teacher, along with any collected assignment papers. Unless you have been requested to correct them, it isn't necessary to do so.

By this time you are able to see for yourself the contrast between subbing in the elementary grades and in the junior high and high school settings. While one demands more of your personal involvement, the other requires objectivity and dispatch.

Depending upon your personality, background, and interests, you may feel drawn toward one or the other. A good sub is valued and respected regardless of the grade levels taught. But for maximum variety and to increase the number of your working days per month, try to be a switch hitter.

PART THREE

A Bag of Tricks

Like a magician who pulls rabbits out of the hat, every sub must have on hand a bottomless bag of tricks; a variety of bright ideas and activities for filling in odd moments or unplanned blocks of time.

Ideally, these activities not only must be fun for the students but should have educational value as well. Practically speaking, they must be simple enough to be pulled out of the bag at literally a moment's notice.

Some subs literally carry such a bag—a lightweight tote filled with such goodies as stories, puzzle books, color by numbers sheets, old magazines, and assorted ready-made timefillers. Often a small bell or whistle is included for efficient attention getting, and sometimes even a few small, inexpensive, or merchant-donated "prizes."

Subs who prefer to travel light almost always carry a stock of timefiller activities committed to memory—impromptu projects and learning games ready to take the stage on cue.

Now you can have the best of both worlds at your fingertips. Carry along whatever makes you feel comfortable. But

*flip through these pages until the paper wears thin, choosing
fun-filled and educational activities selected with you and
your students in mind. Some are old and some are new.
Each has tested kid appeal and needs little or no advance
preparation.*

Have fun.

12.

Timefillers in the Bag

Everybody is the right age for a story. Telling one, aptly chosen and well delivered, is the most time-honored and enjoyable timefiller of all.

Although any time will do, the ideal time to read a story is after lunch when the natives come back restless and tired from a strenuous romp on the playground. Listening quietly helps to slow down their motors and prepare them for the afternoon's work.

Choose picture storybooks for classes through the third grade. Most classrooms come equipped with a good supply. Young children love to study the illustrations, especially if they are colorful and bold. If you can read at arm's length, do so, switching the book from one hand to the other so that the illustrations are always in view. If your eyesight isn't up to that, read a page or two at a time, pausing to give the children a panoramic sweep of the illustrations.

Many kindergartens and some primary rooms have a "story corner," a carpeted area where the children can sit happily at your feet and can see all the illustrations easily. In classrooms where students are seated at desks or tables, it's a good idea to make an occasional circuit through the aisles so that nobody complains, "I can't see!"

For older students choose classic short stories, more sophisticated fairy tales, or adventure stories. I find stories by O. Henry and Guy de Maupassant especially suitable for fifth and sixth graders, although minimysteries and ghost stories are popular too. If you don't have your own favorites, check the Appendix for library-recommended ideas.

Stories should be read with as much expression and characterization as you can muster. Timing is important, too. You needn't be a Barrymore, but children do respond to a bit of theatrics.

Telling the story should not take more than fifteen to twenty minutes—enough to provide a welcome respite, but not long enough to become boring. If time hangs heavily for the afternoon, extend the storytime by having students draw their own illustrations or by choosing volunteers to "act out" the story. Not long ago I read five or six very short Aesop's fables to a fourth grade class. We talked briefly about the moral in each. Then each child selected his favorite and drew a fitting illustration, complete with title and moral. We made a cover page and had a new "book" for the classroom.

Older students like to debate the subtle moral issues in any good story. Who was right? Who was wrong? Why? How might the story have turned out differently? Frank Stockton's "The Lady or the Tiger?" lends itself to all sorts of heated speculation. Choose up sides and involve the entire class in a discussion.

Even if you choose simply to read a story and move on, the hiatus is a satisfying and rewarding one. Storytelling is so popular that many regular teachers read a chapter a day from a classic children's book. Students may tell you, as they file in from lunch, "Mrs. So-and-so is up to chapter eight."

But there are dozens of other good timefillers—word

games, math games, and the like—that take anywhere from fifteen to thirty minutes to play and can involve the entire class or just a few early birds at a time.

Some subs find prizes a good incentive. They stash away posters, pencils, and other promotional giveaways or send for free samples from a variety of sources. There are paperback books available that list hundreds of potential sources of free materials.

Local merchants—lumberyards, party and stationery stores, and others—are often willing contributors of rulers, calendars, and other items that can be used for this purpose.

I prefer to reward my "winners" with special blackboard credit for quick thinking. "Brainteaser Champs," "Word Find Champs," or simply "Quick Thinkers" are good lists to keep alongside the "Superstars." There seems to be something wonderful about seeing one's name go up on the board. With this method, even those who are far from angels and might never make the "Superstars" list can earn recognition that is visible to the regular teacher next morning.

Whether you choose to use prizes or not, here's a collection of tried and true timefillers, some of which you may recognize from your own childhood. Age groups, preparation, and duration are noted for your ease in instant selection.

Rhyming Words

Grade: K–1
Prep: None
Time: 15–20 minutes

For these youngest students the emphasis should be on participation rather than winning. There are no winners in this game.

Call out a simple, one-syllable word like "tree" or "day" or "go." Write it on the blackboard. Call on the first child to quickly name a rhyming word like "see" or "may" or "toe." Continue calling on children in turn for as long as their rhyming capacity holds out.

When a child gets stuck, he chooses a new word to rhyme with and the game continues. Be sure that the chosen words have plenty of rhyming possibilities.

Scrambled Eggs

Grade: 1–3
Prep: None
Time: 15–20 minutes

In this game you must think of a simple word and write it on the board, but be sure to scramble the letters, such as TAB for BAT or RETE for TREE. Call on the children in turn to unscramble the word and call it out. You may have to give a verbal clue, such as "ball players use this" or "it grows straight and tall."

If you wish to keep score, you can give one point for each word unscrambled. If not, continue playing, giving a new word to each child, with as many clues as necessary.

Word Detectives

Grade: 2–6
Prep: None
Time: 15–30 minutes

This is a favorite for any age group and may be played until interest wanes. It's also a great activity to keep early birds busy until the rest of the class completes an assignment.

Choose a phrase appropriate to the season and write it in large letters on the board. Suggestions might be: MARCH WINDS, APRIL SHOWERS, HAPPY HOLIDAYS—even BACK TO SCHOOL or SUMMER VACATION. Or use the title of a story you have read or a study unit the class is working on, like SOUTH AMERICA.

Ask the students to list as many words as they can find hidden in the letters of the phrase. Letters may be rearranged in any order (for example, CAR from MARCH) but may only be used once for each time they appear. Duplicate letters that appear in the next part of the phrase may be used to create a new word.

A sample list might look like this:

MARCH WINDS

| ram | mar | car | war | ward | arc |
| card | dawn | wand | ham | dam | rim |

Set a time limit and use the following rules:

1. three-letter word minimum
2. no names or abbreviations
3. no adding S to make a new word from an old

At the end of the time limit, have the children count their words and put the number in a circle at the top of the page. Be sure they put their names on the papers before passing them in to you.

Older students will have no difficulty coming up with twenty to fifty words or more. Younger ones may be allowed to use dictionaries.

While the class works on its next assignment, check through the papers quickly for obvious mistakes. (If time is a problem, accept the lists at face value without checking.) Name the top three or four word detectives "winners" based on the number of words they've found.

Gossip

Grade: K–3
Prep: None
Time: 10–15 minutes

To begin this game, whisper a phrase into the first player's ear. The older the group the more complicated the phrase should be. Example: "The old red-headed farmer took his goat and sheep to town to trade for an axe and a hammer."

The player to whom you whispered the phrase must now whisper it into the ear of the second player and so on. By the time the message reaches the last player, who must repeat it aloud, it will have undergone some hilarious changes.

You may want to write down the original phrase to compare it against the final one. In addition to being good fun, this is a good lesson in how gossip can distort the facts.

Campfire Stories

Grade: K–3
Prep: None
Time: 15–20 minutes

To play this version of a campfire favorite, write a word on the blackboard—perhaps "boy." The first player must make up aloud the first line of a story using that word. ("Once upon a time a boy went to the fair.")

Now write another word—perhaps "pig." The second player adds a sentence to the story using the word pig. ("He took his pet pig with him.")

Your third word might be "loose." The third player might add, "The pig got loose."

By your continuing to give clue words to keep the story

on the track, the class can create its own story of fun and adventure.

This is especially effective with younger children. For older students you may prefer to give imaginations free rein by dispensing with the clue words. Point to students in turn and do not interrupt unless they are having difficulty. Nobody is out and there are no winners. This is simply for fun.

Suitcase

Grade: 1–6
Prep: None
Time: 15–20 minutes

This is best played standing in a circle, although the students may stand at their seats if you prefer.

The first player says, "I took a trip and in my suitcase I packed an apple." (Use any word that begins with "A.")

The second player must repeat the phrase, adding an object beginning with "B." ("I took a trip and in my suitcase I packed an apple and a book.")

Each succeeding player repeats the entire phrase, adding "C" words, "D" words, and so on as far through the alphabet as they can. Anyone who misses a word is out, and the game continues until the winner with the best memory is found.

If the alphabet is completed, the next player starts a new list, beginning with "A." Now things really get confusing, and a good time is had by all.

Spelling Bee

Grade: 1–6
Prep: None
Time: 15–20 minutes

The old-fashioned spelling bee remains a tried and true

friend, serving as a review for all the spelling words the class has studied this year.

Have the children stand at their seats. Using the class spelling book for reference, give each child in turn a word to spell. He or she must say the word, spell it correctly, and repeat the word.

Alternate easier and more difficult words at random. If a child misses a word, he sits down. Continue the bee until the last few standing can be named "Spelling Champs."

As a variation of this game, use addition, subtraction, or multiplication/division problems, depending upon the age group. Call it a Math Bee and proceed in the same way.

Memory Game

Grade: 1–6
Prep: Little to none
Time: 15–20 minutes

This game may be varied depending upon the age group you are teaching.

With little ones, seat them in a circle, each with a pencil and paper. Collect an assortment of eight or ten classroom objects such as a ruler, pencil, book, bell, and so forth. Display the objects on the floor, in the center of the circle, for two minutes. Then, having the children close their eyes, remove the objects from view. Now the students may have from two to five minutes to draw, from memory, as many of the objects as they can remember.

I prefer not to declare "winners" among very young students. I merely praise each for his own memory and put a rubber stamp of approval or a sticker on each paper.

For older students, list twelve to twenty objects on the board. Leave the list in plain view for two minutes. Then erase the list (keeping a copy) and give the children two or three minutes to list as many as they can remember on their own papers. Winners are those with the longest and most accurate lists.

Math Bingo

Grade: 2–6
Prep: None
Time: 20–30 minutes

Have each child draw a nine-squared game card on a piece of scrap paper, filling in a randomly chosen number from one to fifty (one to one hundred for older students) in each square. A sample might look like this:

30	6	19
15	44	9
55	16	27

Using simple addition or subtraction problems for younger students, and multiplication or division for older, state a math problem clearly—for example, "fifteen plus four" or "six times six minus three." If the answer matches a number on their game card, they put an X through it.

Keep track of the answers to problems you have given by keeping your own list so that winners can be checked. Continue calling out problems until a child has crossed out three numbers across, down, or diagonally, as in Bingo. He is then declared a winner. The game may continue until you have found as many winners as you wish.

The older the group, the more complex your problems may become, combining two or three processes per problem. This is a great way to sharpen math skills and I have yet to find a class which didn't enjoy it.

Word Bridges

Grade: 3–6
Prep: None
Time: 10–15 minutes

Include the whole class for this or use it as a timefiller for your early birds.

Choose a word not longer than eight letters. The name of the current month or nearest holiday might be a good choice. Write it on the board in capital letters reading up and down, like this:

E	R
A	E
S	T
T	S
E	A
R	E

Children must copy this onto their own papers. Now they should begin filling in letters to form real words that bridge the gaps—for example, "E asie R" or simply "E a R." Older children should be encouraged to fill in the longest words they can think of. The first few who complete their word bridges are declared winners.

To make the game more complex, you might assign one point for each letter added and set a brief time limit such as three minutes. Scores may then determine the winners.

This is a quick, entertaining exercise and may be played several times during the day if time permits.

Gift Certificates

Grade: 3–6
Prep: None
Time: 15 minutes

This is a nice activity to initiate shortly before Christmas or Hanukkah, Mother's Day or Father's Day.

Talk briefly about how generous it is to give a gift of yourself rather than one you have purchased. Encourage your students to think of ways they can help around the house that parents, brothers, and sisters might truly appreciate.

Then have them make a packet of "gift certificates" for the recipient that may be redeemed for: one car wash, walking the dog, doing the laundry, reading a story, a free ice cream cone, taking out the trash, or other services.

Categories

Grade: 3–6
Prep: Little to none
Time: 15–20 minutes

This is an old favorite revisited. The most difficult part is having the children draw the game card, a chore you might avoid by using pre-dittoed diagrams that you have drawn, leaving the spaces blank.

With a word such as the name of the month, school, or

season written down the side, and categories of your choice at the top, the prepared game card might look something like this:

	FOOD	FLOWER	ANIMAL	CITY	COUNTRY
A					
P					
R					
I					
L					

Given a time limit of ten to fifteen minutes, students are to fill in as many squares as they can with acceptable answers (a food that begins with A, a flower that begins with A, and so on).

Younger children may be allowed to use reference books for help. Winners are those with the most squares filled in at the end of the time limit.

Me, Myself, and I

Grade: 3–6
Prep: None
Time: 15–30 minutes

On a piece of paper, each child writes down ten facts

about himself—things that help to identify him. Facts to be included might be favorite sports, hobbies, eye or hair coloring, best friends, accomplishments, talents, whether he walks or rides to school, and the like.

The papers are then folded into fourths and placed in a "hat." Choose the papers at random, one by one, and read the facts aloud. Students may raise their hands at any time to guess who wrote the paper. They may not guess their own names.

This is an amusing game just as it is. If you want to find winners, score one point for each correct guess.

Ghost

Grade: 4–6
Prep: None
Time: 15–30 minutes

For this oldie but goodie, children should stand in a circle or at their own desks. The first player begins by saying any letter of the alphabet aloud—for example, "F." The next player adds a letter of his choice, perhaps "A."

The object of the game is to avoid completing a word. If the third player adds "R" to the existing "FA," he has completed a word (FAR) and must accept as penalty an "out." He then sits down.

That third player, to avoid an "out," might add an "M" to make "FAM." The next player is out if he adds "E" (FAME) but cagey if he adds "O," heading for FAMOUS and laying the penalty on someone else. Each time a word is completed, the completer sits down and the next player begins a new word.

The older the children the greater their vocabulary and their staying power. The game continues until three winners are left standing.

Fizz-Buzz

Grade: 4–6
Prep: None
Time: 10–20 minutes

To play this challenging number game, assign the word FIZZ to any number from one through ten (for example, 3) and BUZZ to another (4). Everyone knows the FIZZ and BUZZ numbers before the game begins.

Players, standing at their seats, begin to count off normally, one number per person. But any time the chosen numbers 3 or 4 appear in the count, or any multiples of them, the words FIZZ or BUZZ must be substituted.

This sample game might sound like this:

"One, two, fizz, buzz, five, fizz (a multiple of 3), seven, buzz (a multiple of 4) . . ."

Remember that any number containing a 3 or 4 (13, 14, 23, etc.) or any multiple of those numbers (12, 15, 24, etc.) must be correctly BUZZED or FIZZED, or both, as in the number 34 (FIZZ-BUZZ) or 43 (BUZZ-FIZZ).

This can be a little tricky to keep track of, but children find it hilarious fun.

Time Capsule

Grade: 4–6
Prep: None
Time: 15–30 minutes

For this timefiller children must pretend they are filling a time capsule to be discovered by astronauts of the future.

I like to divide the class into four or five groups for this exercise but it can be done individually or as a class effort.

First make a list of material to be included; facts that give information about the lifestyle of today. A good list might include names of politicians, entertainers, popular movies, books, fashions, slang expressions—anything the class agrees is representative of their culture.

It's fun to read and compare the resulting answers and it gets kids thinking about the world we live in.

Geography

Grade: 4–6
Prep: None
Time: 15–30 minutes

Another old favorite, Geography may be played by the entire class within a reasonable time limit.

Players may stand at their desks or form a straight line at the front of the room. The first player begins by naming a city, state, country, river, or mountain range (any geographical name will do).

The second player must use the last letter of the place just named to start another geographic place name. A sample game might go like this:

1st player—Californi**a**
2nd player—**A**msterda**m**
3rd player—**M**arylan**d**
4th player—**D**es Moine**s**
5th player—**S**acrament**o** . . . . etc.

A player is out, and must take his seat, if he repeats a name previously used or takes more than thirty seconds to think of an answer. Winners are the last two or three players left standing.

The game gets fast and furious but watch out for all those place names that end in "A"!

City State Lotto

Grade: 5–6
Prep: None
Time: 10–20 minutes

To play this game and the variations listed below, have each child make a list—in this case, of ten states.

Now call off a series of cities. Pause long enough between cities to allow the students to find the matching state if it appears on their list. For example, if you call, "San Francisco," they may cross "California" off their list if it appears there. Keep track of cities you call so that game cards may be checked.

The first students who are able to cross off their entire lists are declared winners.

Variations

1. *Language Lotto*—Children list any ten words, choosing any combination of nouns, verbs, adjectives, and other parts of speech. You call out "adjective" or "pronoun," for instance, and they cross out a corresponding word.

2. *Animal–Vegetable–Mineral Lotto*—Children list any ten objects of their choice (carrot, book, elephant). You call out "animal," "vegetable," or "mineral," and they cross out a corresponding word.

*   *   *

As you go from school to school and from class to class you will surely find your favorite games—and so will your students. In fact, the children themselves may be your greatest source for new ideas. But since you may rarely sub in the same class more than a few times a year, don't be afraid of repeating yourself. Become familiar with the games and timefillers you like best and tuck them into your mental bag of tricks.

13.

Brainteasers

Brainteasers, which we discussed in Chapter 10, can be word puzzles, math progressions, or little tests of logic that can be quickly written on the blackboard to be "solved," just as quickly, by the students.

Adding an element of fun to the academic day, brainteasers themselves are an effective means of keeping order in the classroom. They are earned by the class's good behavior and efficient work. They stop if the class demeanor does not merit them.

Since children find the brainteasers fun and challenging and do not want them to stop, peer pressure alone can keep a class working well and quietly without a word from you. Disqualifying one noisy row or table of children from participating in the next brainteaser can shape up that row pretty quickly.

In reality you may use as few as four or five or as many as twenty brainteasers in a given day, depending on the attitude and ability of the class and the amount of discretionary time available. An average of two or three per hour is reasonable.

The total amount of time thus taken from classroom work is no more than five to twenty minutes in all. Yet the reaction from your students each time you say, "Look up—here comes a brainteaser!" will soon let you know that they are a worthwhile few minutes indeed.

Most brainteasers can be solved in a flash. Some require pencils and paper, so you should caution your students to keep them handy throughout the day.

Each time you introduce a new kind of brainteaser, you will have to give your class a brief explanation of what is wanted and perhaps a simple example.

If students call out the answers they risk being disqualified. They are to raise their hands and wait to be called upon. In the case of a tie, all correct answerers will be listed on the Brainteaser Champs list.

In any classroom there will be those students with quick minds who seem to get the answers more rapidly. Try to call on as many students as possible in the course of a day even if you have to ignore some of the hands that generally pop up first.

Keep this chapter handy for ready reference to the fifty or sixty brainteasers that follow. As you may seldom sub in the same room more than two or three times a year, you will probably use your favorites over and over in different rooms and soon they will be committed to your memory.

Start with the simpler ones and you will quickly gauge the ability level of your class. Then you can pick and choose from the more complex examples when the need arises.

We have arranged the brainteasers in this chapter by type, with some indication of suitability to grade level. But don't be surprised if some fourth graders can handle the toughies, while some sixth graders struggle with the simple ones.

In any case, have fun and if you run out, check the resource list in the Appendix for more bright ideas.

Word Pictures

Look carefully at the way these words or groups of words are arranged. Each stands for a well-known phrase. You must examine not only *what* is written but *how* it is written in order to find the clues.

Here's an easy example: $T_{O_{W_N}}$

Answer: Downtown

* *Teaching Tip:* Many of these are more difficult than they seem (if you don't peek at the answers!). Offer them only to fourth through sixth graders unless you have an especially capable second or third grade class.

Ready? Answers on following page.

1. $\dfrac{\text{man}}{\text{board}}$ 2.   ban   ana   3.   dice   dice

4. $\begin{matrix} \text{d} \\ \text{deer} \\ \text{e} \\ \text{r} \end{matrix}$ 5. $\dfrac{\text{O}}{\begin{matrix}\text{PHD}\\\text{MD}\\\text{DDS}\end{matrix}}$ 6. $\begin{matrix}\text{F}\\\text{R}\\\text{I}\\\text{E}\\\text{N}\\\text{D}\end{matrix}$ STANDING $\begin{matrix}\text{F}\\\text{R}\\\text{I}\\\text{E}\\\text{N}\\\text{D}\end{matrix}$
MISS

7. $\dfrac{\text{wear}}{\text{long}}$ 8.   gettingitall   9. $\dfrac{\text{man}}{\text{moon}}$

129   Brainteasers

10. C
     A
     P
     T   N
      A I

11. LAL

12. flying
     c   c
      c^c c
      cc

13. po FISH nd

14. belt
     hitting

15. | reading |

16. age   beauty

17. ground
     feet   feet
     feet   feet
     feet   feet

18. death   life

19. head
     heels

20. M   L

     E   A

21. time   time

22. throwing
     hand

Answers to Word Pictures

1. Man overboard
2. Banana split
3. Paradise

4. Deer crossing
5. Three degrees below zero
6. Misunderstanding between friends
7. Long underwear
8. Getting it all together
9. Man on the moon
10. Captain Hook
11. All mixed up
12. Flying overseas
13. Big fish in a little pond
14. Hitting below the belt
15. Reading between the lines
16. Age before beauty
17. Six feet underground
18. Life after death
19. Head over heels
20. A square meal
21. Time after time
22. Throwing overhand

Word Ladders

Word ladders are two like or unlike words connected on a "ladder" with three blank "rungs" in between. An example might look like this:

WARM

———
———

———

COLD

The idea is to change one letter of the top word to form a new word (WARM to WARD). Then change one letter of the new word to make another new word. Repeat the process, changing one letter to make a third new word. By changing one letter of this word, you should end with the word at the bottom of the ladder. The finished example might look like this:

> WARM
> WARD
> CARD
> CORD
> COLD

    * *Teaching Tip:*   Word ladders are most suitable for fifth and sixth graders. Try them on capable fourth graders.

RATS	LOSE	RISE
RATE	LONE	RILE
MATE	LINE	RILL
MITE	FINE	FILL
MICE	FIND	FALL

WALK	BOOK	LOVE
WALL	BOON	DOVE
MALL	BORN	DOTE
MALE	WORN	DATE
MILE	WORM	HATE

Math Progressions

Math progressions are a logically ordered sequence of numbers with a blank at the end. Students must first find the pattern and then fill in the blank. An obvious example:

> 2 4 6 8 __ (10)

132   A Bag of Tricks

* *Teaching Tip:*   Math progressions may be used for any age group if you are careful to select mathematical concepts with which students are familiar. The example above is quite suitable for first and second graders. Choose some from the examples below. Then make up your own progressions for whatever grade you are teaching.

1   6   3   8   5   __   (10)
(add 5, subtract 3, add 5, subtract 3, etc.)

2   4   8   16   32   __   (64)
(multiply each successive number by two)

9   18   27   36   45   __   (54)
(the nine times table)

256   64   16   4   __   (1)
(each number is divided by four)

3   9   6   18   15   __   (45)
(times 3, minus 3, times 3, minus 3, etc.)

56   49   42   35   __   (28)
(the seven times table backwards)

Analogies

For this type of brainteaser you must give your students a brief lesson in analogy, or comparing the relationships between things. Teach them the symbol : which stands for the words "is to." Write this example on the board.

Sacramento: California as _____ : New York.
The blank word must be "Albany." California and New

York are states. Sacramento and Albany are the capital cities.

In addition to giving experience with analogies, a part of many standardized tests, this type of brainteaser will challenge students to recall different kinds of information about many subjects, depending upon the analogies you choose.

* *Teaching Tip:* Analogies may be used successfully with all grade levels. Use information within their mastery. Young children might handle analogies like these:

Green : grass as _____ : sky.   (blue)
Brother : sister as _____ : girl.   (boy)
Mustard : hot dog as _____ : pancakes.   (syrup)
Sun : day as _____ : night.   (moon)
Paw : dog as _____ : person.   (hand)

For older children choose analogies like these:

Motorcycle : policeman as _____ : witch.
  (broomstick)
Drape : window as _____ : person.   (clothing)
Honolulu : Hawaii as _____ : Georgia.   (Atlanta)
Vine : grape as _____ : apple.   (tree)
Ink : pen as _____ : car.   (gasoline)

The possibilities for drawing analogies are endless. Make up any number of your own, using information from subjects the class is now studying.

After doing several analogies with the class, you just might challenge students to write a few of their own. The first student finished, with acceptable analogies, gets his name on the Brainteaser Champs list, too.

Word Math

Word math brainteasers "add" or "subtract" words to form new concepts. A simple example might be:

Bees + nectar = _____ (honey)

or

Trees − many leaves = _____ (autumn)

* Teaching Tip: A quick study of the subject matter taught in various grade levels will give you lots of ideas for your own word math brainteasers.

For very young children, try:

Clowns + elephants + trapeze = _____ (circus)
Cows + chickens + pigs = _____ (farm)
Bread + peanut butter + jelly = _____ (sandwich)

For older children choose more complicated ideas:

Senate + House of Representatives = _____
   (Congress)
Society − government = _____ (anarchy)
Canada + U.S. + Mexico = _____ (North America)
Three angles + three sides = _____ (triangle)
Inspiration + expiration = _____ (breathing)
Orange − red = _____ (yellow)

Children like these word math ideas and get the hang of them quickly. You might ask them to make up some of their own based on social studies, English, and math terms they are presently studying.

Logic

Logic brainteasers may be divided into two types. The first, which children of all ages can do, points out the similarities and differences between any two things. Example:

Name some ways in which a box and a bag are alike.

1. They may both hold things.
2. They may both be squares or rectangles.
3. They both have three letters in their names.
4. They are both often brown in color.
5. They may both be made of paper.

or

Name some differences between a turtle and a bird.

1. One has wings and one has legs.
2. One moves quickly, the other slowly.
3. One has a shell and one does not.
4. One can live in water and one cannot.
5. One has feathers and one does not.

The second type, more suitable for older children, sets up a problem in which clues must be found and used to draw a logical answer. For example:

There are two kingdoms side by side. One may import such things as oranges, umbrellas, amplifiers, eggs, and ink. The other may import only such things as pencils, books, spaghetti, radios, and dishes. Why?

ANSWER: One kingdom imports only items which begin with vowels, the other only with consonants.

Mary wears dresses of red, blue, and yellow. Linda wears dresses of orange, pink, and aqua. How do they choose their clothes?

ANSWER: One chooses only primary colors, the other only secondary colors.

Goofy Grammar

Brainteasers of the Goofy Grammar variety are simply sentences or paragraphs you write on the board which contain numerous errors in spelling, punctuation, and grammar.
The children must find and correct the errors, on paper. The first student turning in a neat and correct version gets his name on the Champs list.

* *Teaching Tip:* These brainteasers are suitable for every grade level as long as children have begun to read and write. Use imagination, and choose interesting topics. Write the incorrect sentence or paragraph on the board.

Examples for first through third grade might look like this:

tom and tina go two skool
me dog spot playz with mee
may i have too cookies

Older children might wrestle with paragraphs like this:

my freind george and me went too the dessert for the week end we sleept owt onder the stars witch was fun but it was to hot to sleep anyways george got a nice tan but i got burnt luckaly we fowned some medecine

to sooth the burn and we had fun on sunday wouldnt
you have fun on your own two

A simple variation of Goofy Grammar is to mix up the
words within a sentence and have the children straighten
them out:

Is Egypt the Cairo capital of
Sides every four square equal has
New years elect we president four every a

14.

Instant Arts and Crafts

In my travels as a sub I have seen, in various classrooms, towers built of toothpicks, delicate and dazzling arrays of string art, and a vast collection of intricate design work worthy of the label "art." The creativity of some imaginative and dedicated teachers never fails to amaze me.

Yet the fact of the matter is that arts and crafts can run the gamut from simple drawings to complicated construction projects that require lots of advance preparation and materials.

For those of you with true artistic talent, supervising a unique art/craft activity can be the highlight of your day—and the children's. No matter the age group, youngsters are captivated by the infinite capacity of color and the pure possibility inherent in a single sheet of paper. By all means, use this fascination to inspire good communication, wonderful behavior, and pride of craftsmanship. The children will be proud to take their work home.

But those of us with three left thumbs and an artistic flair that ends with the deft tossing of a salad must bear in mind that arts and crafts of any kind are among the most valued and valuable trinkets we can pull out of our bottomless bag of tricks. To cap a successful day or save a faltering one with an absorbing craft project is to elevate yourself to the ranks of the Super Sub.

One lesson we can learn is the value of simplicity. Our time with each class is limited. There is rarely opportunity to glue one day and paint the next or to explore fully the elaborate processes of pottery. If your forte is clay, you must be satisfied with a none too perfect batch of pinch pots and consider yourself successful if the children have learned a little and incidentally had a good time.

Resources and materials are similarly limited, so we must content ourselves with presenting snappy little projects that can be completed with ease and speed and do deliver an interesting finished product.

Don't let me discourage you if you can draw, from your own experience, some unique and fanciful art projects to share. Your expertise will be much appreciated and the kids will jump for joy when they see you coming.

For the rest of us, here is a potpourri of what I call instant arts and crafts: projects requiring little time, talent, or preparation that can spark the interest of your students with nothing more than the garden-variety materials found in nearly every classroom. There are greeting card ideas, paper sculptures, collages, and more, as well as tips about age groups and necessary materials. The approximate time required is noted, too.

You may want to try some of the paperfolding yourself to be sure you have the hang of it before presenting it to your students. I can guarantee you from the limited dexterity of my own left thumbs that they are simple. Soon you will be a relative expert whose classes clamor for more. So choose your favorites—and happy crafting.

Collage

Grade: K–3
Time: 30–60 minutes
Materials: An assortment of your choice

I have listed this activity as suitable for the little ones because, as an experiment in form, color, and texture, it is particularly appealing to young children. However, using more sophisticated materials and design work, it can be just as absorbing for older students.

Construction paper, paste, popsicle sticks, paper clips, paints, or crayons and such are standard in most primary rooms. But to make full use of this project—and you will, often—begin to collect your own scrap materials and carry them with you to class.

Include such items as buttons, macaroni, small scraps of fabric, bits of yarn and ribbon, seeds, sequins, and toothpicks. As you begin to master the art of collage new ideas will occur to you all the time.

Give each child a sheet of white or colored construction paper. Spread an assortment of your available materials in the center of each work table. Paste or white glue is essential. The children may pick and choose items to their heart's content, pasting them onto their papers to form their own designs.

Show the youngsters how to coil a bit of yarn before gluing it on, how to arrange "flowers" using buttons for the centers and seeds, ribbon or macaroni for the petals and stem. Help them cut tulip or butterfly shapes from fabric scraps, adding stems, leaves, or stamen from other materials.

Encourage them to use their own pattern ideas and to trust their sense of color and dimension. For as long as your materials hold out, this is a sure-fire winner for the little ones. For older children, suggest a combination of collage and crayon art. They can create whole scenes, capping a crayoned mountain with seed or cotton "snow" or filling a sketched-in brook with leaves and pebbles.

Shape Art

Grade: K–3
Time: 30 minutes
Materials: Art paper, colored paper, scissors, paste, crayons, or felt tip markers

While a "helper" is passing out art paper and the children are getting out their colors and paste, quickly cut out some geometric shapes from the colored paper. Use simple triangles, squares, rectangles, and circles, none larger than the size of a half dollar.

Put an assortment of shapes in the center of each table and let the children select the ones they want to work with. Before they begin to paste, however, show some simple examples of shape art.

Show how a triangle can become a clown's hat and a circle of another color his face. The triangle could be a stick figure's dress, a rectangle the body of a dog. Encourage the children to "see" the shapes as something other than just circles and squares.

Once they have decided what their picture will be, they may paste on the shapes and draw in the features and details to complete it. The older the students, the more imagination they will display and the more fun they will have with this activity.

Number Drawings

Grade: K–3
Time: 15–30 minutes
Materials: Art paper, felt marker, crayons

This simple exercise can be lots of fun and a great imagination stretcher, too.

Give each child a piece of art paper and, moving from one child to the next, ask him to choose a number from one to nine. Using your felt marker pen, draw his number two to three inches high right in the center of his paper.

Now ask the children to "see" the number as the body of their drawing. A "one" can be the beginnings of a tree, a "three" the body of a snowman. A "five" can be the beginning of a whale, a "seven" the spoke of a windmill.

If you study the shapes of the numbers yourself, you will have no difficulty suggesting possibilities to anyone who is "stuck."

Paper Weaving

Grade: K–3
Time: 30–40 minutes
Materials: Construction paper, scissors, rulers, pencils

This is great practice in measuring and cutting, though kindergarteners will need close supervision.

Each child will need two different-colored sheets of construction paper. On the first, draw vertical pencil lines one ruler-width apart. Cut along each line to within one inch of the border.

On the second sheet, draw horizontal lines one ruler-width apart and cut into strips. Have the children trade some strips with neighbors so that each ends up with a variety of different colored strips.

Now they weave the strips into the first sheet by pushing each strip in and out of the cut-out lines in a horizontal direction. Alternate strips begin over and under the first cut-out section.

The result is a colorful checkerboard placemat which the children may use at their desks or take home.

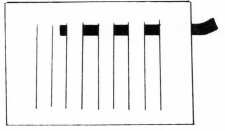

Pipecleaner Art

Grade: K–3
Time: 20–30 minutes
Materials: Pipecleaners

Don't forget about pipecleaners! They come in a terrific assortment of colors and are inexpensive items to carry in your bag of tricks.

They can be bent and twisted into an infinite variety of shapes and patterns limited only by imagination. Stick figures, animals, flowers, and balloon bouquets are but a few suggestions. Children never tire of the possibilities and, what's more, pipecleaners can be reused time and time again.

Paper Bag Masks

Grade: K–3
Time: 30–45 minutes
Materials: Grocery bags, crayons, scissors

I don't know about your house, but in mine the paper grocery bags stack up faster than you can say "dirty dishes." Now, instead of tossing them into the trashbin, I grab an armful when I'm off to the primaries.

With a strategically placed pair of holes for eyes—you do this chore, please!—they make wonderful masks of every description, from robots to Indians to glamour girls. Drawing and coloring in the features fills many a happy minute for children. When you're finished, how about a parade of masks or a skit with these ready-made characters?

Paper Flags

Grade: K–3
Time: 30 minutes
Materials: Construction paper, scissors, crayons, staples or masking tape

Speaking of parades, here's a dandy idea for a project. Each child can design his own flag.

Fold one sheet of construction paper into nice, neat quarters. Unfold. Cut away the lower right hand section. The upper right hand section becomes the flag and may be decorated in any manner the child desires.

When the flag is designed, the upper and lower left hand sections become the flagpole or stick. Simply roll it into a nice, tight cylinder and fasten with staples or tape.

Children may be encouraged to draw flags of all nations or to depict their own hobbies and interests.

Children of All Nations

Grade: K–3
Time: 40–60 minutes
Materials: Art paper, scissors, crayons

For this variation on a row of hand-holding cutout dolls, fold a sheet of white art paper into accordion pleats about three inches apart. After folding, draw a paper doll figure making sure that the arms, legs, and top of head extend right to the edges of the paper.

Cut out the doll through the entire thickness of folds. Unfold to reveal your chain of brotherly love. Direct the children to decorate each figure with costumes and facial features of all nations, using encyclopedias or reference books for ideas.

Holiday Bells

Grade: K–3
Time: 20–30 minutes
Materials: White art paper, scissors, white glue, crayons, paper clips

Cut circles approximately six inches in diameter. Ask each child to decorate his circle in any manner he chooses.

Make one cut to the center of each decorated circle. Pull the cut sides together and overlap the edges to form a cone. Glue the edges together and hold with paper clips until dry.

At home, the paper clips can be removed. Mom can insert a piece of yarn or string through the tiny top opening so that the decorative bell may be hung and admired. If time permits, each child can make a cluster of bells, each with a different design.

Paper Snails

Grade: K–3
Time: 15–30 minutes
Materials: Construction paper, scissors, white glue

Mark the construction paper into one-inch-wide strips and cut. Give each child one or two strips.

Show them how to pull the strip carefully but firmly right along the edge of the tabletop until it curls. They now have the body of the snail.

Fold one end under to form the head. Draw on a happy face and glue on tiny curls for antennae.

Try it. It works!

Crayon Etchings

Grade: All
Time: 30–45 minutes
Materials: Art paper, crayons, paper towels, paper clips

Have students cover the entire paper with blotches of bright crayon color in any random pattern they choose. When finished, rub or "polish" the paper all over with a paper towel (available in most classrooms.)

Now, have the children cover the entire paper surface with black or any dark colored crayon, totally obscuring the bright colors underneath. Polish the black layer with a paper towel.

Finally, with the opened end of a paper clip, have them scratch (etch) a design or picture through the black coating down to the color. The effect is rather like stained glass.

Thumbprint People

Grade: All
Time: 20–40 minutes
Materials: Art paper, inked stamp pad, colored pencils or
        felt tip markers

My twelve-year-old daughter, Stacy, came up with this idea, which has become a favorite with many classes. The beauty of it is that while the little ones can do very simple pictures the older kids get detailed and imaginative!

To begin, press each child's thumb onto the inked stamp pad (available in most classrooms) and have him "print" two or three thumbprints on his paper. These thumbprints will form the "heads" of the people he draws.

Now the students can use their imaginations to draw in facial features, bodies, and details in various sports, dance, or other poses.

The cutest one I ever saw showed two tennis players facing each other across the net, complete with sweat bands and little droplets of perspiration.

Greeting Cards

> *Grade:* All
> *Time:* 20–60 minutes
> *Materials:* Art paper, crayons or felt tip markers, sometimes scissors or white glue.

Nearly every school month has its own excuse for a greeting card—everything from Halloween to Father's Day. Since children of all ages enjoy making their own cards, choose from the ideas here to help them create original and interesting designs.

For the simplest cards they merely fold the paper in half so that it opens like a book. They decorate the covers and put the messages inside. For added interest you might hold a contest for the most original or clever verse or greeting.

For more interesting cards, have the students fold the paper into thirds, folding the outer two thirds in toward the middle. Now both covers can be suitably decorated, opening to reveal the message inside.

An even more unusual card can be created with some extra paperfolding. This may require some patient instruction but the results are worth it for fourth through sixth graders.

Since most art paper is rectangular in shape, we must first come up with a square. This can be accomplished with a ruler and pencil but there is an easier way:

Fold corner A toward the bottom of the paper until it meets point C and the bottom edges are even. You have now formed a triangle. By cutting away the excess along the right side you will have created a perfect square.

Unfold and hold the square on the diagonal so that it resembles the shape of a diamond. Carefully fold each corner in toward the very center so that the corners meet exactly.

Now you have a three-dimensional card with all sorts of possibilities for decorating borders and flaps, revealing a message inside.

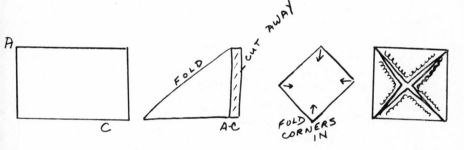

For an interesting decoration on any plain card, have the children cut out shapes (hearts for Valentines, eggs for Easter, bells for Christmas, and so on). They color the entire outer edge of each cut-out shape with brightly colored crayon. Then they lay the cutout on the paper or greeting card and, using a finger, gently smudge the crayon border onto the card with short, straight movements all around. Remove the cutout and the silhouette is now on the card.

Holiday Ideas:

For Valentines, invest in some inexpensive round paper doilies and have the children glue on bright red cut-out hearts. Or create a pattern of different sized red hearts glued onto white art paper.

At Easter, cut out good-sized egg shapes and have each child decorate one. Then direct him to cut the egg in half with a jagged horizontal cut so that it looks as if it had just cracked open. Glue both halves onto contrasting paper with space for a message between the cracked halves.

For Mother's Day, have the children cut out flowers from different colored papers and glue them onto white art paper, collage fashion, to create a bouquet. Stems and leaves may be cut from green paper and glued on for added decoration.

Decorative Chains

Grade: All
Time: 20–40 minutes
Materials: Construction paper, scissors, stapler or tape

Rena Guinnare, a teacher at Workman School in the Covina Valley Unified School District, showed me this terrific idea for decorative paper chains just right for festooning around the room. Although she assures me that "everybody knows it," it was new to me, and it may be to you.

Children cut construction paper into four-inch-wide strips

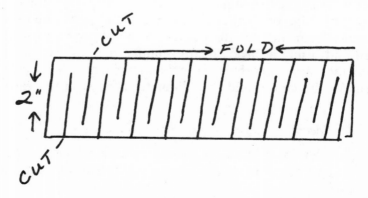

and fold each strip in half lengthwise to form a folded two-inch strip. Beginning at one end, alternating sides for each cut, they cut nice, straight lines through to within one-fourth inch of the edge.

When the entire strip has been cut as illustrated, they open up the fold and stretch the strip gently to reveal this intriguing chain. Strips can be stapled or taped together to make longer chains. Easy, isn't it?

Picture Frames

Grade: 3–6
Time: 10–15 minutes
Materials: Construction paper, scissors, pencils, paste

A sixth grader taught me this wonderful idea for creating shadow box frames in which to display those lovely drawings your class has made.

First, center the drawing on a piece of construction paper that is one or two inches larger all around than the drawing. Draw a pencil line around the picture and remove it.

Fold in each edge exactly on the pencil line. Now, pinch each corner together to form a shadow box effect and paste in the drawing. *Voilà!*

Paper Sculpture People

Grade: 4–6
Time: 30–40 minutes
Materials: Art paper, scissors, crayons or felt tip markers

This is a super project for a class studying brotherhood or international relations, although any group will enjoy it.

Have each child choose a nation and find a picture of the national costume in an encyclopedia or textbook.

Students fold a piece of art paper in half. Starting at the fold, they draw half the outline of a doll with the approximate shape of the intended costume, being sure to leave a wide base or "platform" under the feet.

Have the children cut along the outline of the folded paper, open it flat, and draw in the facial features and color the costume. When decorated, the figure stands on its own wide base, which is slightly folded or attached to another piece of art paper for a three-dimensional poster effect.

Note: If you prefer, the class may use storybook or other imaginary characters for these figures.

Mirror Image Drawings

Grade: 4–6
Time: 30–45 minutes
Materials: Old magazines, art paper, scissors, colored pens

A sixth grade teacher at Cypress School in Covina clued me in on this one. Kids seem to love it, but it does require lots of old magazines.

Have each child cut out a picture of his choice from a magazine. It may be a face, a can of beans, a jug of wax, a luscious dessert—anything that strikes his fancy. It must be cut out carefully so that it retains its entire shape.

The students fold the desired picture in half lengthwise, cut along the fold, and paste the left half of the picture on a piece of art paper. (Left-handers may want to paste on the right half.)

Now, as closely as possible, using the other half of the picture for reference, draw the missing half onto the art paper as though it were the mirror image.

Draw and color in the details, making the mirror image

complete. This is a challenging and absorbing project often worthy of those shadow box picture frames when complete.

Dot Graphics

Grade: 4–6
Time: 30–50 minutes
Materials: Art paper, pencils or felt tip markers

From Polly Swirsky of Ben Lomand School in Covina comes this idea for innovative graphic design.

Direct the students to draw five or six dots, at varying heights, along the width of the art paper. Using symmetrically curved lines, they begin to connect the dots. They must use carefully curved lines, always starting in the center of one dot and ending in the center of the next.

When the paper is filled in this manner, the children color in the crescents in a random or planned color pattern.

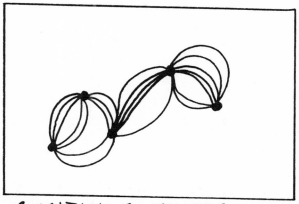

CONTINUE CONNECTING
FROM ONE DOT TO
NEXT UNTIL FILLED.

Geometric Designs

Grade: 4–6
Time: 20–30 minutes
Materials: Art paper, scissors, paste

My fourth grader, Michael, brought this idea home from his teacher, Nancy McMullen at Mesa School. While it is hardly a new idea, it is one which is well worth remembering. Michael can vouch for the enthusiasm of his classmates.

To create these unusual designs, no two of which will be alike, the students start with a piece of art paper and fold it into eighths. With scissors, they begin cutting out a series of wavy lines or differently shaped holes in any random pattern. They must cut through the entire thickness each time.

When the paper is unfolded they will find a symmetrical geometric design closely akin to Indian art or snowflakes. They can paste the result onto art paper of a contrasting color for a truly beautiful effect.

Patchwork Art

Grade: 4–6
Time: 30–45 minutes
Materials: Art paper, crayons or felt tip markers

My daughter won a coloring contest using this lovely, mosaiclike technique.

I often have my students draw the outline of their hand on the art paper as a coloring base. At Easter the shape of an egg may be used, a heart shape for Valentine's Day, and so on.

Using wavy pencil lines, the children divide the shape

into a series of "patches" so that the end result looks something like a jigsaw puzzle.

Now they fill in each patch with a different, tiny pattern in varied colors. They may use stripes, crosshatch, polka dots, tiny hearts, diamonds, or paisleys—anything that appeals to them. The finished design looks like a fragile patchwork quilt.

Like the sixth grader who taught me how to make shadow box picture frames, there will always be children who can improve on your designs and add new ones to your repertoire. Listen to their good ideas, for who knows better the sort of arts and crafts that children like best?

Be alert to samples of artwork posted in the classrooms you visit. Good ideas are everywhere for the sub whose eyes are open, and whose intention it is to make the most of an hour and some papers and crayons.

15.

Creative Play

Children are the greatest natural actors in the world. They begin early to imitate parents and friends in a comical or mock serious and often all-too-accurate manner. If you've ever watched a five year old scold her naughty dollies or recreate the entire cantina scene from *Star Wars,* you know what I mean.

As their little psyches develop, however, and they become sensitive to the reactions of their peers, they often fall victim to shyness and inhibition. No longer are their imaginations given free rein.

Exercises in creative play help them to rediscover, in a socially approved way, the joy of self-expression. The purpose of these exercises in the classroom is not to unearth latent Bernhardts or Oliviers, but to cultivate awareness of the world around us and to foster understanding of the universal human emotions.

Furthermore, acting is fun. While no one should be forced to participate, most children welcome the opportunity to volunteer. As a substitute teacher you will rarely have the time to stage a play, although there are excellent anthologies of scenes and excerpts in the library. But simple exercises in creative play are popular and worthwhile timefillers to haul out of your now bulging bag of tricks.

The term creative play covers a whole spectrum of playacting exercises in which we use our voices and/or our bodies to communicate ideas and feelings. Basically, these experiences fall into three main categories as they are applied to the classroom: pantomime, improvisation or role playing, and dramatization.

Pantomime means body language. It is the art of showing emotion or situation without the use of words, by using exaggerated bodily movements. An act of pantomime can be as simple as opening an imaginary door or as complex as pretending to change a tire. It is important to pay close attention to the detail of every action so that others can understand what we are attempting to show.

Children like pantomime because it gives them the chance to "show off" without the embarrassment of having to use words. An impromptu pantomime session in the classroom is always greeted with delight.

Improvisation or role playing involves ad-libbing words or dialogue in order to act out or solve a given situation or problem. The situation must be set up in advance: "You are trying to convince your mother to let you go to a rock concert with your friends." All the "parts" or characters are represented by the children, who make up their own dialogue as they go along.

Role playing helps children to understand both sides of a problem; to see the other person's point of view. A child playing out someone else's role gains conscious awareness about motivation other than his own—about what makes the other guy tick.

In a sixth grade classroom not long ago we were reading a chapter of a health textbook that dealt with family relationships. In the text, a girl borrowed her sister's sweater without asking permission. In the course of the day she got an ink stain on it. When she returned the ruined sweater the sister flew into a rage and the parents came running to prevent mayhem.

"Oh, wow!" muttered one of my students. "Sounds just like my house."

"Yeah," said another. "I once broke my brother's baseball trophy and I thought he and my Dad were both gonna kill me!"

"What could you have done differently to prevent that situation?" I asked.

"Run away from home?" he suggested. The class broke into laughter.

"Wait a minute," I said. "Let's play it out and see." Assigning the roles of the siblings and the parents, we put the family "on stage." For an absorbing half hour we tossed the situation around, each "actor" bringing something new to the scene. I don't know that we ever fully solved the problem but giving the kids a chance to get into someone else's skin, so to speak, certainly helped to broaden their understanding.

Often there is some giggling and silliness when you set up your first improvisation. It's embarrassing to lay feelings out in the open. But as the children get caught up in their own dramas, they begin to respond with enthusiasm. Sometimes it's their only forum for self-expression—a rare and valuable commodity. The trick is to set up situations that are meaningful to the students.

Dramatization differs from role playing in that it may use an actual script, as in play- or scene-reading, or perhaps the story or situation being dramatized is "fictional"—that is, more removed from the actual lives of the kids.

A story you have read to the class may be dramatized. The roles of Pinocchio, Gepetto, and the other characters are assigned to the children who will then act out the story. Students through the third or fourth grade particularly enjoy this. For older children a dull history lesson can really come to life when the adversaries actually take the stage.

Whichever methods you choose to use, I think you'll find creative play exercises wonderful tools for heightening class involvement and interest. With this in mind, here are some ideas that you and your classes can explore and enjoy together.

Five Senses

Grade: K–3

These exercises provide a wonderful introduction to pantomime for young children.

Talk for a few moments about the five senses we all possess—hearing, sight, taste, touch, and smell. Let the answers come from the students. Get them thinking about facial expressions we all use when our senses are affected. Then have volunteers come up in turn, and whisper to them an example of something that indeed affects their senses. Using only gestures and expressions, they must now convey this to their classmates.

Some examples to get you started:

1. Smell something burning on the stove.
2. See a newborn kitten on the playground.
3. Hear a sudden noise outside.
4. Taste a new vegetable for the first time.
5. Feel paste stuck to your fingers.
6. Touch something very hot.
7. Smell your favorite dinner cooking.
8. See a surprise for you at the dinner table.
9. Hear music being played too loud.
10. Taste a yummy birthday cake.

*   *   *

Now ask the children to think of and act out other examples of things that affect our senses. Call on volunteers for as long as their imagination and interest hold out.

Fun with Rhymes

Grade: K–1

The purpose of this exercise is to act out familiar rhymes, combining song and movement.

Have the children stand in a circle. Choose a "farmer" for "The Farmer in the Dell." As the children sing the song the farmer chooses a wife, the wife chooses a dog, and so on. Each child chosen must act out the character he or she is supposed to be.

Now try "Old MacDonald Had a Farm," "Jack and Jill," "Little Miss Muffet," "Little Bo Peep," and other popular nursery rhymes until the class's interest wanes.

Just before you stop you may want to teach the children this singsong rhyme, if they don't already know it.

> Five little monkeys
> Jumping on the bed,
> One fell down and
> Hurt his head.
> Mother called the doctor.
> The doctor said,
> "No more jumping on the bed!"

The verse continues with "four little monkeys," then "three," and so on until all the monkeys are gone. Young children seem to love the mischief in the lyrics and the singsong rhythm. Choose five monkeys, a mother, and a doctor and have the children act out the "story" as the class sings along.

When I Grow Up

Grade: K–2

Ask the children to think for a moment about some things they might like to be when they grow up. Help them to picture the kinds of physical movement that go along with each job. "Think to yourself," you might suggest, "what actions a person in this job performs. What tools does he or she use in his or her job?"

Now call on volunteers to act out their chosen professions slowly and with as many details as they can think of. Repeat the actions if necessary until classmates can guess the right job.

You might start them off by pantomiming a teacher yourself. Open a book, walk to the blackboard, pick up an imaginary piece of chalk, and pretend to write.

If the children get stuck, you may call for volunteers and whisper suggestions to them: baseball player, nurse, golfer, doctor, basketball player, fireman, and others.

Introductions

Grade: K–3

In this exercise, volunteers must "introduce" their imaginary friends to their classmates. These friends may be real people, animals, or even favorite toys.

You may want to do the first one as an example. "This is my friend, George. He is small and soft. He has bright eyes and lettuce is his favorite food. He has long ears. He likes to hop." Stop when hands go up in the air and the guesswork begins.

Ask for volunteers to introduce their "friends," naming as many facts about the friend as possible until the children guess who or what is being introduced.

Remind the children that some good facts to use are size, coloring, favorite foods, hobbies, what the friend likes to do, and where he or she lives.

You might think that children are discouraged if their "friends" are guessed too soon. Actually, the reverse is true. They seem to feel most successful when introductions are rapidly recognized. And after all, a feeling of success is what we're after with creative play exercises.

Pantomime Fun

Grade: K–6

Pantomime actions can be enjoyed by children at all grade levels. The actions can become more complex for use with older students. The main thing to remember—and to remind your class—is that all pantomime actions must be done clearly and slowly, using as much detail as possible.

Start by pointing out to the children how we all use some of the same pantomime actions every day, like wrinkling our noses when we don't like something or pulling back a hand when we touch something hot. Facial expression is much the same world over. Our faces can signal how we feel and our bodies can suggest actions that others can recognize without words.

Do a simple pantomime yourself, such as cracking an egg into a skillet. Now choose volunteers and whisper suggestions to the first few. Some examples might be:

1. Fill a glass with tap water and drink.
2. Open a birthday present.
3. Give an imaginary speech.
4. Set the table for dinner.
5. Learn how to juggle.

6. Put a leash on your dog and take him for a walk.
7. Mix up a cake.
8. Look for something that is lost.
9. Play a guitar.
10. Taste something which is too hot.

Older children can be given more complicated situations involving both action and emotion:

1. Tear open a letter and find good (or bad) news.
2. Try to find someone in a crowded airport.
3. Watch your favorite team win (or lose) the game.
4. Come home with a bad report card.
5. Put on a costume and make up for a show.
6. Blow up a balloon, tie it, and then watch it pop.
7. Watch your favorite TV show and the set poops out.
8. Burn yourself while ironing a shirt.
9. Dig into your favorite food.
10. Get impatient while waiting for someone to show up.

The possibilities are endless and once the kids get the hang of it, they will be very creative onstage. Soon your students will be setting up and pantomiming their own ideas so that you can get in on the guesswork.

Improvisations

Grade: K–6

Like pantomimes, improvisations can be enjoyed by students at any age. The key is to set up role playing situations which are meaningful to them and applicable to their particular age groups. Many successful improvisations involve conflict of opinion or desire.

Learn to spot class lesson work that lends itself to improvisation, such as a current events report or a question on which the children do not agree. Assign the roles of the conflicting parties and let them play it out, working out solutions that grow out of their discussion or "dialogue." Or, just for the fun of it, set up some situations for role playing yourself.

For younger students, try these:

1. Two children are arguing over a toy when Mother comes into the room.
2. You want to go outside and play but Daddy says it's too cold today.
3. You find a puppy and bring it home but Mom says you can't keep it.
4. You want to borrow your brother's baseball glove but he doesn't want to lend it to you.
5. Three children are trying to convince each other to watch their own favorite TV show.
6. You were not invited to a birthday party and Mom tries to make you feel better.
7. A new baby has been getting all the attention and you complain to your parents.
8. You have hurt your best friend and now you want to apologize.
9. Try to convince your older sister and her friends to take you with them to the movies.
10. Convince your teacher that you have a good reason for not having done your homework.

Suggestions for older students:

1. You are babysitting for the first time and can't persuade the five year old to go to bed.
2. You want to get a part time job but your father thinks your schoolwork will suffer.

3. You see your friend shoplift something and you try to persuade him (her) to put it back.
4. You want to learn to ski but Mom thinks it is too dangerous for you.
5. You are upset because you lost a swimming competition and your friend tries to cheer you up.
6. Club members are trying to decide on the best way to raise money.
7. Three friends each have their own ideas about how to plan a party.
8. You have broken your sister's favorite necklace and now you must tell her about it.
9. You fixed dinner for your family. They are all eating, but you know it tastes awful.
10. You forgot to mow the lawn and now your Dad threatens to take away your privileges.

Charades

Grade: 4–6

This old party favorite is easily adapted to the classroom. It takes only a few minutes to explain the common charade gestures: "little word," "sounds like," "on the nose," "six words," "two syllables," and so forth.

You will simplify the game by choosing to use only book titles, famous quotations, popular songs, or any single category at a time.

To play charades, divide the class into two teams, one on each side of the room. Give each team a few minutes to make up five charades for the opposing team. They must write them down and put them in a "hat."

If there is an odd number in the class, appoint one child timekeeper. If not, act as timekeeper yourself. At the timekeeper's signal, volunteers from each team must act out the charades submitted by the opposing team while their team-mates try to guess the answer within a three minute time limit. Keep track of time used by each team for each of their five charades.

The winning team is the one that uses the least amount of time to get their messages across.

Silly Speeches

Grade: 4–6

This exercise is wonderful for helping children learn to speak comfortably before groups. It also happens to be a favorite timefiller activity among my older students. Because it is so silly by nature, it seems to spark their imaginations and inspire confidence in their ability to speak without fear of making a mistake.

You will simply call on volunteers to make one-minute "serious" speeches on silly topics such as these, which you can write on the blackboard or pull out of a "hat":

1. Whale blubber: Newest taste sensation!
2. The care and feeding of robots.
3. Training pets to do your work for you.
4. Abba Dabba Land: A new vacation paradise.
5. The world's most perfect food: figs.
6. Germs need love, too!
7. Building a Foofnagel from scratch.
8. World's best teacher explains secret of success.
9. How to find a fortune in your garbage pail.
10. Dingleball! The newest rage in sports.

Debates

Grade: 5–6

Debating teaches children to organize their thoughts and to make convincing presentations. In order for them to have real impact it is important, as with improvisations, that the issues being debated are of genuine interest to the class.

Unlike Silly Speeches, debates require of the speakers conviction and knowledge of a very real subject. Debates may grow out of a class discussion or they may stem from issues you present.

Offer a choice of three topics for debate. Note which evokes the most response from the group. Ask for volunteers to represent each side of the issue and select four or five debaters for each team.

Debaters have a two-minute time limit in which to state their arguments clearly. The rest of the class will then vote on which team was most convincing.

The idea behind this exercise is less to instill the basics of true debate than to encourage youngsters to take a stand and argue it respectably. Some possible topics for debate are:

1. Should students have a say in determining their own grades?
2. How important is education in today's world?
3. Which is more important: Good health or riches?
4. Should TV watching for children be limited?
5. Should movies have ratings?
6. Cheating: Is there ever a good excuse?

When leading creative play exercises of any kind, keep the interest level of your class uppermost in mind. Continue them when participation is good and be prepared to stop when interest wanes. Their greatest value lies in promoting spontaneity and understanding in an atmosphere of good fun. When fun deteriorates to silliness, it's time to ring down the curtain.

16.

Indoor Sports for Rainy Days

Kids cooped up in the classroom all day are like popcorn expanding in the popper. Without the release of recess, play time, and physical education the popper is apt to pop its top. When bad weather precludes this release, the result can be disastrous. Tempers flare, attention lags, and a general unrest sets in. What to do?

The answer, of course, is to provide some sort of steam valve. Energy spent in running and playing means more relaxation and concentration in the classroom.

Those of you who sub in areas where gymnasiums are part of the school scenery can fall back on basic indoor sports like basketball and volleyball.

In California, where the sun always shines (?) and in other areas where good weather is the norm, gyms are often a thing of the past. A single structure serves as lunchroom/auditorium, with no provisions made for indoor sports. The first few drops of rain send us scurrying to our rooms where a little ingenuity about indoor sports is a valuable and worthwhile commodity.

The games and exercises presented here all involve physical movement. If you do have gym facilities available they can act as a supplement to other activities. If you don't, they can be a lifesaver. True, they can never really take the place of regular, outdoor exercise. But they can provide a much-needed steam valve when the alternatives are seatwork or chaos.

All of these indoor sports take space limitations into account. They are divided into two main categories, Relays and Games. Attention is given to their suitability for the K–3 and 4–6 grade levels.

P.S. Even if the sun shines all year long, try them just for the fun of it.

RELAYS

Relays are team activities. They are races, of a sort, that pit two or more teams against each other competing for top honors. Some relays require more physical agility than others. Some are truly humorous to watch and fun to participate in.

I like relays because the emphasis is on team, rather than individual, prowess. There is ample opportunity to root for one's teammates and to use lots of pent-up energy.

Since anywhere from eight to twelve children can make up a relay team, you will probably want to divide your class into thirds. If you are faced with an odd number, choose one or two children to act as "Relay Directors" who can keep a close watch on the proceedings to be sure all the rules are being met. If you try more than one relay the directors should be rotated so that everyone has a chance to play.

It's not a good idea to pit the boys against the girls. The best way to choose teams fairly is to count off, "One, two, three," while pointing to each student in turn around the room. All the "ones" form one team, all the "twos" another, and the "threes" a third.

Line up the teams at the starting line, forming three straight rows. Explain the rules of the relay you have chosen. In each, every team member will have to complete the same given task, as must all members of the opposing relay teams.

With your "Ready, set, GO!" the teams begin their tasks and the team completing the relay first is declared the winner.

K–3 Relays

Somersault Relay   At the signal, the first child on each team must do a series of somersaults from one end of the room to a given point at the other end. Having reached his goal, he then runs or somersaults back to tap the next of his teammates on the shoulder and goes to the end of the line. Each teammate tapped in turn completes the same task until one entire team finishes first.

This relay may be played equally well using hopping, skipping, or jumping as the mode of travel.

Wheelbarrow Relay   This is a partnership relay in which each child on every team has a partner. At the signal, one partner lies on the floor face down. The other partner lifts the legs of the first, wheelbarrow fashion, so that the child on the floor rests on his hands. The partnership, maintaining this wheelbarrow position, races down the relay trail and then back to the team, where the next partnership takes over.

Blackboard Art   At the signal, the first member of each team runs to the blackboard, picks up the chalk, and draws the head of a person on the board. When he runs back and taps his next teammate, the second child runs up and adds part of the body. The third may add arms, the fourth, legs, and so on until the whole person has been drawn and all the players on each team have had a turn.

If there are a lot of members on each team, the last players may be adding hats, shoes, belts, or other articles of clothing until the team is finished and the chalk person is completed. This in itself can get pretty funny. One enterprising second grader, while the opposing teams struggled with shoes, hats, and gloves, merely drew an umbrella so that his teammates could each draw one spoke!

Relays for All Grades:

Book Walk   At the signal, the first member of each team balances a book on his head and walks the length of the room. He walks back, still balancing the book on his head, and gives the book to his next teammate. Each child on the team completes the task until one team finishes first.

If a player drops the book at any time during his walk, he must return to the starting line and begin all over again.

Calisthenic Relay   Any calisthenic exercise may be selected for this task. For example, the first player on each team runs to the head of the classroom, does three push-ups (or sit-ups, or whatever you choose), then runs back to tap his teammate, who repeats the exercise.

Older children may be directed to do a series of calisthenic exercises, which they must remember to perform in the correct order.

Shoe Relay   This one always becomes a favorite. Before starting, each child removes his right shoe and places it in a pile at the front of the classroom.

At the signal, the first member of each team runs to the pile, finds his shoe, puts it on correctly (shoelaces tied and all). He then races back to tap the next player and the relay continues until one team wins.

Over and Under   For this relay, give a large rubber ball to the first child on each team. At the signal, the ball is passed back over his head to the next player. That player passes it between his legs back to the third player.

The ball is passed over and under in this manner until the last player has it. The ball is then started back to the front of the line in the same way. The first team to have the ball back at the starting line is the winner.

Pass the Peanuts   Gather up an unwieldy handful of objects for each team—perhaps two erasers, several books, a jacket, three pencils, and a ruler. Give these "peanuts" to the first player on each team.

At your signal, the "peanuts" are passed to the player behind him and so on down the line. Eventually, they must be passed forward again. Any player who drops the "peanuts" must gather them up again before passing them to the next player.

The winner is the first team to successfully pass the peanuts all the way down the line and back again.

4–6 Relays

Blackboard Sentence   This is a variation of the blackboard art relay upgraded for older children. In this version, the first player on each team runs to the blackboard and writes the first word of a sentence—any sentence. The word might be "The" or "Once" or any word that appeals to him.

When he runs back to tap his teammate, that player must run up and add a word to the sentence. The relay continues until all players have added a word, regardless of the length of the sentence.

If this seems too simple for your group, have the first player write an entire sentence and each succeeding player add a sentence, so that the result is a story on the blackboard.

Birthday Relay   At the signal, all team members must ask questions and rearrange themselves in line in the correct order of their birthdays. In other words, if the first birthday on the team is January 15, that person would be at the head of the line. He or she would be followed by the next birthday in order, with December at the end of the line. The first team to rearrange itself in the proper order is the winner. Sounds easy, but try it.

A variation of this relay is to have the students rearrange themselves alphabetically by either first or last name. It's a great exercise in alphabetizing, and it's fun.

Math Relay   In this relay, each team depends upon the math capability of its members in order to win. The first player runs up to the board and writes a multiplication problem with at least two digits in each number. The second player must work the problem on the board and come up with the correct answer. The third player writes a division problem for the fourth player to solve.

Alternate multiplication and division problems, being sure that they are not too easy for the group's ability. You might decide to add one digit each time a new problem is written, making the tasks successively more difficult.

First team to employ all of its members successfully is declared the winner.

GAMES

Games lack the element of team competition that relays provide and that so many youngsters have come to expect in their recreational activities. However, they do provide a combination of physical activity and rhythm that most children seem to enjoy.

Some of the games suggested here, particularly those for older groups, do designate "winners" by a process of elimination. I try to end the games with a group of winners rather than with one or two people. Games suggested for younger children generally do not have "winners" at all. Their emphasis is on group fun and activity rather than on individual prowess.

Included are old favorites and new variations, listed by suitability for various age levels. Most can include the entire class at once. If there is not enough space to arrange the whole class in a circle when required, you may choose to play a series of games, including half the class each time.

By their nature, these games can supply the physical activity you need on a rainy day. At the same time, they are versatile and brief enough to be used in the classroom anytime you feel a break from routine is in order.

Games for K–3

Looby-Loo   Many youngsters will recognize this old verse or can learn it quickly. They all seem to enjoy the movement. To play, arrange the class in a circle, standing. Begin singing the chorus, having the children join hands and walk to the center of the circle, then out again. As each verse is sung, use the appropriate "action" to match the lyric.

176   A Bag of Tricks

Chorus: Here we go Looby-Loo,
Here we go Looby-Light,
Here we go Looby-Loo,
All on a Saturday night.

Verse: I put my right hand in,
I take my right hand out,
I give my right hand a shake, shake, shake,
And turn myself about.

Sing the chorus between each verse. The verses, in succeeding order, involve the left hand, right foot, left foot, and whole self.

Face to Face   This game requires an uneven number of players, with one person acting as "It," while the rest of the group chooses partners. If you have an even number in your class, you must play and start out as "It." In a group of an uneven number, the extra child is "It" and you merely supervise.

To play, the partners stand together, grouped randomly around the room. "It" stands to one side. At the signal, "It" gives commands to the partners, such as "face to face," "back to back," "left hand to left hand," and so forth, which the partners must obey.

When "It" commands, "All change!" everyone, including "It," must get a new partner. After the shuffle, the child left without a partner becomes the new "It."

There is no stigma to being "It," because "It" gets to give the commands.

Fruit Bowl   Seat the children in a circle, with or without chairs. A leader stands in the center. Each child in the circle is given the name of a fruit in the fruit bowl—pear, apple, banana, orange, plum, and grape.

The leader begins the game by giving commands like,

"Apples change with pears" or "Bananas change with grapes." At the command, children bearing those fruit names must make the commanded change of seats. When the leader calls out "Tip the fruit bowl!" everyone must change seats.

Each time the positions change, the leader tries to find a seat. The child left without a seat becomes the leader and the game continues.

Tricky Hot Potato   In the traditional game of Hot Potato, the children stand in a circle passing an object like a ball or an eraser from one child to the next around the circle while music is played on a record player or piano. Each time the music stops, the child holding the object is out and is eliminated from the game until a winner is left.

In Tricky Hot Potato, no one is eliminated. Instead, if a child is left holding the object when the music stops, he continues to play—but with the tricky penalty of having to pass the object backward or over his head or under his knee. Everyone must remember his penalty and use it each time the ball comes his way.

Continue playing until the children are doubled up with laughter over the "tricks" they must now perform.

Games for Everyone

Trashcan Basketball   This game closely resembles a team sport, if you want to appoint teams. It can be played just as happily by the whole group at once.

You will need a large rubber ball to play with and an empty wastepaper basket for a "basket." Depending upon the age of the children playing, set the basket from five to fifteen feet away from the youngsters lined up at the throw line.

Each child in turn has three chances to make baskets by

tossing the ball into the can. To count, it must not bounce out.

One point is given for each basket scored and you may or may not decide to keep track of the points to find winners. The fun of the game is in making baskets, not in finding a winner.

Simon Says For this old favorite the children may stand at their seats or in any given area. The leader, either you or a designated student, faces the group.

The leader gives a series of commands. "Simon says, touch your nose," "Simon says, put your hands on your hips," "Simon says, raise your right hand." Everyone must obey the command if the phrase "Simon says" precedes it.

If the leader says, "Touch your toes," without "Simon says" preceding it, then the command must not be obeyed. Anyone who responds to a command without "Simon says" is eliminated and must sit down.

The game may be made easier or more difficult by slowing down or speeding up the commands. The sting of being "out" may be alleviated by choosing a new leader every few minutes from among the children who have been eliminated.

Follow the Leader Students may remain in their seats for this game or may be seated in a circle on the floor. A Guesser volunteers and is sent from the room. Meanwhile, a Leader is selected from among the group remaining.

When the Guesser returns, the Leader chooses a motion such as slapping the knee, pulling an earlobe, clapping hands, or patting the top of his head. Everyone follows the Leader by repeating the same motion. The Leader must change motions every few seconds, with the whole group following suit.

The Guesser must try to name the Leader by watching closely. When the Leader is found out, he becomes the

Guesser and he leaves the room while a new Leader is chosen. Play for as long as you like.

Games for Grades 4–6

Air–Water–Fire The group stands in a circle. "It" stands in the center of the circle with a ball or blackboard eraser. "It" tosses the ball to someone in the circle, calling out "Air," "Water," or "Fire."

The player to whom the ball is tossed must catch the ball and, if "Air" or "Water" is called, quickly name a creature (animal, fish, fowl, or insect) who lives in that particular element. If "Fire" is called, the player remains silent, tossing the ball back to "It," who tosses the ball to another player and calls out a new element.

If a player fumbles the ball, repeats a creature already named, or breaks the rhythm by delaying the ball, he is out and changes places with "It."

Who Am I? To play this delightful game (I have used it successfully at adult parties!), give each child a slip of paper on which to write the name of a well-known person, living or dead. Suggest that they choose actors, presidents, rock stars, athletes, and so on.

All the names are dropped into a "hat" and mixed up. One by one, each child comes up to the teacher, draws out a name without looking at it, and the teacher tapes it to the child's back.

When all the students have been "labeled," they may wander about the room asking questions of their classmates in an attempt to learn who they are. All questions must be answerable by "yes" or "no." (Am I male? Am I blond? Do I sing? Do I make speeches? Am I younger than thirty?)

If a child thinks he's discovered who he is, he checks with

the teacher for confirmation. If correct, he is a winner and his label is removed. He may continue answering questions for other classmates who are still trying to learn their identities.

Depending upon the time available and the interest generated, the game may be played until any number of winners are determined.

Categories Seat the players in a circle on the floor. Show them the following rhythm: slap thighs twice, clap hands twice, snap fingers once. The resulting sound should be "slap, slap, clap, clap, snap." Practice this for a minute or so until everyone gets it right. It is important that the rhythm not be broken.

When you are ready to begin, on the first "snap" the first player chosen names a category (for instance, states, flowers, birds, fruits, vegetables, presidents). The rhythm continues unbroken.

On the second "snap," the second player must name something in the category the first player chose. (If "states," for example, he might say, "Florida.") The rhythm continues.

Every time a "snap" is heard, the next player in turn must name something in the category. If he misses the beat, repeats a name, or gives an incorrect answer, he is out. The next player in turn, at the sound of another "snap," names a new category, and the game continues for as long as you wish to play.

After you've tried a variety of the relays and games suggested here, your own favorites will emerge. As you become adept at gauging your classes in terms of interest and proficiency you will have no difficulty in matching the activity with the group.

And be alert and receptive to suggestions made by your students. You may pick up your best new ideas in just that way.

17.

Using Your Own Special Talents

I know one sub who's a natural-born storyteller. The man has traveled extensively and, through the years, has built up a seemingly endless stock of anecdotes about the places he's seen and the people he's met in his travels.

Furthermore—and this is important—he tells his stories with such humor and imagination, and with such vivid imagery, that he can keep a class spellbound and literally begging for more.

This man's entire bag of tricks rests on his experience and his talent. Whether filling in a spare twenty minutes until band practice begins or an entire lunch hour forced inside because of rain, he merely perches on the edge of the desk and transports his students to parts unknown.

He metes out doses of history, geography, and social studies in the guise of enthralling travelogues. His classes are orderly, his popularity assured, and his value as a sub much reknowned. How much schoolwork is being accomplished is a question I cannot answer. But without a doubt he works very regularly, because he is able to keep his students happily occupied.

Of course, not all of us can be storytellers or can travel the world as he has done. Yet the fact is, there are probably as many ways to be a really good sub as there are personalities walking around this Earth of ours. Each of us brings to the job a unique combination of interests and experience that forms the basis for our techniques and our success.

The key is in recognizing our strengths and talents and in using them to everyone's advantage. Whether your background is in lion taming or doll collecting, find a way to make it useful as a sub.

In the first place, you are never more comfortable than when you talk about something you know and like. Remember—enthusiasm is contagious. Children are eager for new interests and piqued imaginations. They are a willing and ready audience.

In the second place, your special interest in wildlife or music can give your classes a bright, new perspective—an enjoyable "elective," if you will, that might otherwise never be introduced. No knowledge is wasted. An intriguing foray into the area of your special interest may not only provide a needed timefiller, but may be just the ticket to keep you in control and your classes in apple pie order.

A cheerful young sub I spoke with recently carries her guitar with her on all her assignments. It is, first of all, an object of great curiosity, resting splendidly against the blackboard as the children file in. Many youngsters have never seen a real, full-size guitar at such extraordinarily close range.

Early in the day—often right after the Pledge of Allegiance—she suggests an appropriate song. She strums the chords on her guitar as the children sing. "How many of you can play a guitar?" she asks. Few hands are raised. "How many of you would like to?" Nearly every hand in the room goes up.

"If we can get our work done quietly and well," she says

now, "we'll make some time to sing. Some of you will even learn how to play." She is true to her word. The children are captivated. Taking "song breaks" throughout the day, she chooses well-behaved youngsters and teaches them the chords. Her classes are wide-eyed, eager, and well organized.

Another sub, proud of her cactus garden, uses its fascination in her work. The star attraction in her bag of tricks is a stock of tiny paper cups, a sack of potting soil, and a non-spiky cactus plant ready for cuttings.

She baits the hook with a promise to have a "planting bee" later in the day if the class is well behaved and efficient. Sure enough, when the work is done, each child gets a chance to plant his own cactus. They talk about the unusual plant and about other desert life. They talk about cactus care and cultivation. Everyone decorates his cup container and takes his new "pet" home.

Lil Robin, presently in her twenty-fifth consecutive year as a sub in southern California, has been transporting a menagerie for years. A nature enthusiast, she has carried tortoises, hamsters, banty hens, even bunny rabbits to school, much to the delight of her students.

Once, she says, she neglected to cover the cardboard box in which she carried a family of tortoises to school in her car. Some babies had been newly hatched just in time for first grade. When she arrived at school, Lil found that Papa Tortoise had somehow taken a stroll. She finally found him wedged beneath the driver's seat, and the custodian had to do some carpet surgery before the family could be introduced to the class.

As always, the tortoises were a huge success. The children fondled, fed, and learned all about the breeding and hibernation habits of this fascinating reptilian family.

"We've always had small animals at home," says Lil. "They're a source of wonder for children. Having them in the classroom keeps the kids interested, eager, and well behaved so they can share in the care and feeding."

Transporting animals, plants, or musical instruments to school can get a bit cumbersome at times. Yet each of these successful subs has found a way to integrate their interests and talents into the job they do.

What source of wonder—what aspect of your personality—can you stash into your bag of tricks? What prize in the package that is uniquely you can be valuable in your work as a substitute?

Begin by examining your hobbies. Those spare time activities to which you naturally gravitate are a storehouse of ideas and possibilities.

Do you sew? Cook? Golf? Garden? Naturally, you will not want to take a sewing machine to school, or a microwave oven and a host of ingredients. But there are activities you can build around your hobby that involve only a little preparation.

Every seamstress has a bag full of scraps—fabrics, trimmings, extra buttons, and such. What a wonderful way to use them! With a package of needles and a few spools of thread you are prepared for a super handicraft. Demonstrate a simple overhand stitch. Let each child practice on a scrap. Now have them sew change purses, comb- or pencil-holders, or other small projects with materials you have on hand. Buttons and trims can add to the fun and you'll have a very absorbed class. Even boys through the fourth grade will enjoy this homely task, especially if you have some vinyls in your scrap bag.

When your own stock begins to wear thin, check with a local fabric or variety store. Explain your purpose and you may be surprised at the stuff they are willing to donate. Upholstery and drapery shops can be a great source of free materials. They often discard outdated sample books.

I once walked into a craft shop just to look for craft ideas. I explained my purpose as I browsed around and the owner came up with a surprise. It seems he'd been shipped a few dozen plaster of Paris figurines slightly damaged in the transportation. He intended to dispose of them as the manufacturer suggested rather than pay the cost of returning them. Could I use them as a project for students?

The damage turned out to be barely noticeable and he even threw in some jars of paint. My idea shopping turned into an unexpected bonanza that kept a third grade class happy as clams one rainy, minus-lesson-plans afternoon. Now I mention my subbing duties wherever I shop. While the trunk of my car sometimes looks like a traveling garage sale, I never lack for interesting things to do.

Apart from materials happily donated, there are hobby projects that cost next to nothing. You don't want to invest a sizable chunk of your hard-earned paycheck, but a dollar or two may be worthwhile.

A gardener can work wonders with watermelon seeds, or peach and avocado pits. A packet of flower seeds costs fifty cents. Tiny paper cups are cheap. So is potting soil if you can't get it free. Work up an hour's activity in which kids draw pictures illustrating seed germination, learning as they go. Cap the hour with a planting session and instructions for care and transplanting. Weeks later, children will hail you excitedly in the parking lot. "Guess what? My tomato plant is growing!"

Recipe ingredients can be costly. For that reason you may not want to "cook" regularly in class. But you do know a lot about nutrition. What games can you devise, perhaps along the lines of bingo, about sorting foods into their proper nutritional categories?

My children's dentist keeps a display of little pill bottles in his office showing the amount of sugar contained or "hidden" in various types of food. Can you prepare a similar display or chart, using it as the basis for a lesson or a game?

As a special treat, perhaps in bad weather or when you expect to have time on your hands, thumb through your cookbooks for no-bake cookies, granola, or "gorp" that the children can prepare early in the day and enjoy after lunch or while you are reading a story. Or let it be known that "Superstars" will be selected to do the mixing and fixing toward the end of the day, while the others watch and learn, and perhaps even copy the recipe. Then the treats can be distributed for everyone to take home a sample.

In my experience, markets won't generally donate ingredients. However, they often give a discount for food purchased for school use. Check it out if this is your forte.

A friend of mine who decorates cakes for her own pleasure sometimes shows her students how to make little "squeeze bags" from waxed paper. Then, using a tinted cream cheese frosting she carries in a plastic bowl, she has them write their own names right on the backs of their hands. The result can be admired and consumed at will, although if a child prefers not to eat it, he is free to wash it off.

And speaking of the backs of hands, I know a man who entertained his own children by painting puppet faces on his balled-up fists. As a sub, he sometimes shows the children how to do this with washable felt tip markers on their own hands, using the thumb as a moveable "mouth." He splits the class into small groups who then take thirty minutes to produce a short skit to present to the rest of the class.

These are certainly novel ideas and they wouldn't work for everyone. But they point up how inventive people can be with the hobbies that interest them most.

Charts and posters can be very handy to present material that interests you especially. Depending upon the subject matter, check with bookstores, libraries, and professional organizations, which may have old displays gathering dust in the storeroom.

Camera buffs can use their own photographic displays—

slides or even homemade movies. (If you require anything other than sixteen millimeter projectors, carry your own equipment.) Do choose your subject with children in mind. They won't sit still too long for travelogues of mountains and rivers. But if the places you have photographed feature people in foreign settings, with lots of color and costume and character, they may be very worthwhile as teaching aids.

Collections can be another potential source of interest, although a word of caution is needed. First, be sure the collection is of interest to children. Rocks and geodes, seashells and sand dollars, for example, fall under the heading of "small wonders." Children like to touch and examine them. A stamp album, on the other hand, may hold far less intrigue unless you can relate it to large maps or other visual material and devise an absorbing presentation.

Secondly, think more than twice about taking valuable collections to school, or items that are somewhat fragile. The responsibility is wholly yours and it isn't always easy to watch out for nimble hands or clumsy, curious fingers.

The same is true of equipment you bring in order to share your hobby with your students. A sub in northern California carries golf clubs and whiffle balls (never real golf balls—they can be dangerous) and gives golf lessons to her students during P.E. It goes over well since this is a sport not usually available to children at least until high school. Another sub sets up croquet matches. In both cases, the equipment is sturdy and easily kept track of, and safety is easily managed. Apply these criteria to any equipment you consider taking to school.

Of course there are many subs who prefer to travel light, unencumbered by supplies and equipment. They rely, in great measure, on their own ingenuity and on the kinds of timefillers we discussed earlier. But they are quick to spot the opportunity for a bit of fun during or after a lesson.

They know the value of a break from routine when it comes to maintaining interest.

These subs are often lively personalities who are aware not only of their personal magnetism but of the kinds of things to which children respond.

It isn't necessary to be a pied piper, nor is that always desirable. I heard of one sub who drove a shell-pink taxi cab and prided herself on her eccentricity. Unfortunately, her students were more bewildered than bewitched and the pink taxi cab is no longer in evidence.

Do rely on your natural sense of humor and on your ability to get along with people. Children are little people, after all. They will enjoy your wit and spontaneity. They thrive on occasional little anecdotes just like anyone else. Most of all, they appreciate a pleasing personality. They are much more apt to be well behaved and responsive if you are relaxed and having a good time than they are if you repress your own personality for the sake of what you think are the "standards."

After all, why do so many children "fall in love" with their teachers in the first place? Because they are distinct and honest personalities who relate to their students with interest and humor and tact. A sub does not have weeks or months in which to foster a complex relationship. But certainly you stand a far better chance if you can share what you are with your students.

My own fourth grader recently fell into a mud puddle at school. He must have been dripping and quite a sight because the secretary called me at the school where I was subbing that day. Needless to say I was helpless to do much about it from a distance of five miles away. I hung up the phone, chagrined but amused at the picture he must have made.

My fourth grade class, who had heard every word, were now eager for all the details. As it happened, their classroom music lesson had just been canceled and we had half an hour to fill. Breathes there a kid, I thought, who cannot relate to a mud puddle there for the jumping? So we spent an amusing, productive half hour writing stories about how the incident might have happened and drawing some humorous illustrations.

Writing is my special interest, of course, and I encourage it whenever I can. I seized on the moment, the interest, and the timing and made it work for me. Artist, square dancer, rock hound—what?—make it work for you.

And if some of the ideas I've talked about here seem to place you in the role of entertainer as much as teacher, perhaps there is an element of truth in that. Remember, you are filling in for the regular teacher, often in a different classroom every day.

When there is a detailed lesson plan to follow, you will do your best to keep the classroom activity much as it would be if the teacher were here. You will teach the lessons and supervise projects to the best of your ability.

Without a lesson plan, however, you must depend on your special talent. You do not have the teacher's stock in trade from which to draw, nor can you second-guess what lesson or activity he or she might choose to initiate. Neither, as a stranger without the power of the grade, can you expect to maintain order and interest with quite the same authority.

What you can do—in fact, what you must do—is to fill those empty minutes with the most interesting variety of educational sorcery you can conjure from your trusty bag of tricks. If you can do it with flair and unlimited enthusiasm, you will hold the attention of your students.

In my travels through several school districts I have met subs who are quiet and low-keyed and subs who are walking dynamite. In my correspondence with subs nationwide I've found backgrounds of every description. Yet the universal feature—the common ground that each of these successful people shares—is a keen awareness of who they are and a willingness to share it in their work. And they do work, happily and regularly, often far more than they'd bargained for.

Supplement the suggestions in Part Three with projects based on your expertise. Together they will furnish the grist for your mill, provisions for your own bag of tricks. Use them. Infuse them with your personality to make your job as a sub hassle-free.

PART FOUR

Where Do I Go from Here?

A movie star was approached on the set by a young, ambitious bit player. "How does it feel to be a success? To have all your struggles behind you?"

"To tell the truth," replied the star, "it's the biggest problem I've had."

"How can you say that?" the newcomer persisted. "You've made it. You're right at the top!"

"That's the problem. If I'm at the top—where do I go from here?"

Good question. Success breeds its own complications, including the question of what to do next.

For many, subbing is an end in itself; a source of pride and income for as long as they care to pursue it. For others, it is a stepping stone to another kind of teaching career.

Whatever your goals when you started out, Part Four is about your success. It begins with a critical self-evaluation and suggestions for making a good thing even better. It continues with ideas for growth and sharing. And the curtain comes down with a potpourri of "helpful hints" from the stars of this particular show—teachers, subs, and kids.

18.

A Chart for Self-Evaluation

A sixth grade teacher I know schedules conferences with each of her young students about two weeks before the end of each grading period. The purpose of these conferences is to allow the students to evaluate their own work and to recommend what they feel is a fair grade in each area of study.

"Kids come into my classroom," she says, "with great glee and a lot of self-confidence. They know, from my reputation, that they will have a say in their grades. And although I'm not bound by their recommendations, I find more often than not that we are in pretty close agreement." A mischievous smile dances across her face. "In fact, if anything, they tend to be a lot harder on themselves than I would be!"

Little wonder. For in spite of our desire to succeed—to convince the other guy that we have put forth our best effort—when all is said and done, there is truth to the adage that we are our own worst critics. No one knows better than we how we rate in our own performance.

But recognizing the extent of our success, as this canny

teacher knows, is only the beginning. Perhaps the more important task is to analyze where our weaknesses lie and to make the effort to improve them. This, then, is the focus of our self-evaluation: to determine the value of the job we've done and to plan for the necessary improvements.

Don't attempt to make this judgment until you have been subbing on a fairly regular basis for some months—perhaps near the end of your first school year. In this part-time career we learn by doing. We make mistakes and we learn from them. It seems hardly fair to judge success on the basis of too short a training period.

Yet as the school year comes to an end, or certainly before a new one begins, we feel the need to stand back and have a look at exactly what we have been doing. Has the year been gratifying and productive for us? Have we fulfilled our obligations?

If we were actually to prepare a chart, it might include the following four questions:

1. Am I happy in my job as a sub?
2. Am I working as much as I'd like?
3. Am I earning enough money?
4. Am I requested by teachers and principals?

The answer to each is important in its own right. Together, they lead to some inescapable conclusions. Let's examine them one by one and see what patterns emerge.

AM I HAPPY IN MY JOB AS A SUB?

Happiness is a relative thing. Possibly you'd be happier rich and not having to work at all. Or maybe, given your druthers, you'd elect to be a movie star at least. So for our purposes, let's define happiness as satisfaction with the job as it is and satisfaction with the way we handle it.

If, by June, you tremble every time the phone rings and would rather climb Mt. Everest in your bare feet than face another classroomful of children, something is definitely wrong. We will presuppose here a certain willingness to work and a reasonable anticipation of each day.

Now if you have reservations about answering with a straightforward "yes," where does the problem lie?

Are you uncomfortable with the material you teach? Do you sometimes feel it is beyond you? Nothing can undermine confidence like not knowing the answer, and it's difficult to waltz into a new room cold to face equations you haven't seen in years.

As a writer I have a lot of confidence in my ability to string a sentence together correctly. But my confidence comes from years of experience. Specifically pointing out the adverbial clauses or indirect objects can admittedly give me pause.

Fortunately, curriculum does not vary much within the same grade level or from year to year. Once you have been through a trial by fire, you are apt to remember the curriculum clearly. The more experience you have with a subject, the more proficient you soon will be.

Consider your familiarity with details of the curriculum a part of your on-the-job training. If you aren't prepared in a specific area, sidestep that lesson in favor of another, or teach an aspect of it with which you are familiar. Assume that the material will become second nature to you after your initial exposures. Assume, too, that the lessons you substitute are of equal value in the whole great scheme of education.

If seventh grade algebra sends you into a tailspin, request your assignments in the lower grades or in other areas. You don't have to take everything that comes your way, you know. You may decide to buckle down to an independent refresher course and tackle that algebra class when you feel ready.

The same may be said of discipline and control, if this is where you feel you are weak. There is a knack to handling older students and no dishonor in admitting you aren't up to it. Concentrate your efforts in the lower grades until (if ever) you are comfortable about moving up.

Perhaps yours is the opposite problem. You try to accept whatever assignment is offered but first grade rudiments are dull and boring and "he took my pencil!" drives you up a tree.

For your own benefit, try to recall the classes you've taught in which you've been the happiest. If a pattern of primaries or high school classes appears, by all means stay within those areas. Ultimately, success in one area may move you to tackle others. If not, then you have at least found your subbing "home" and there's nothing wrong with that.

Are you dissatisfied with the time flexibility—with never knowing how much free time you'll have with a class? This is a problem that comes with the job, but gets easier as your expertise grows. It might be simpler to follow a detailed lesson plan all the time, but often it's not nearly as much fun.

Become thoroughly familiar with a range of timefillers. Look for ways to correlate them with the curriculum. Introduce your favorites at your own discretion rather than at the mercy of the timetable. It's a rare teacher who will mind your taking liberties with the lesson plan if you've had a productive day. The more relaxed you are about rearranging a day, the happier you will be. Don't get so carried away with having fun, however, that you neglect the necessary work—and correction.

Perhaps your unhappiness is not with the classroom at all, but with the subbing system itself. Erratic time shuffling bothers you. You don't feel comfortable with the faculty. There's never another sub to talk to. Familiar complaints, all. Ah, but this is the trade-off for free-lance teaching—

and there are ways to change the system.

In the last analysis, who among us is entirely happy in our work? From the lowliest errand boy to the guy at the top of the corporate heap, everybody knows a better way! Everyone can think of things to change. If you have suggestions for making the sub's life a better one, share them with your district personnel. If you can't get anywhere on your own, read Chapter 19. Your ideas can count.

And if the answer to "Am I Happy?" is at least a qualified yes, congratulations! We need lots more like you.

AM I WORKING ENOUGH?

"Enough," too, is a relative term. To be fair, let's equate the word "enough" with the approximate number of days per month you had hoped to work when you accepted the job.

If the answer is "yes," wonderful! You need only to decide whether to try to increase your work days, decrease them, or allow them to remain the same. If you haven't worked as often as you'd hoped, why not?

Are there too many subs available in your district, reducing your opportunities to be assigned? If so, consider registering in other nearby districts as well. Remember that, in some cases, it may even be possible, with the proper certification, to cross state lines. The more districts in which you are registered, the more frequently you will be called.

Are you accepting assignments in as many grade levels as you can? What about special classes? The greater the range of the classes you are willing to teach, the greater your opportunity. Unless you have valid reasons for restricting yourself to primaries or high schools, you may need to broaden your goals.

Are you turning down too many assignments? Is the temptation to sleep late or to take visiting Aunt Martha to

Disneyland getting in the way of your professional goal? Can you drop a daytime class and pick it up in the evening? Can you swallow your timidity about tackling upper grades and begin to accept their beckoning calls?

Whether you are refusing assignments on the basis of personal or professional reasons, you are doing so at the expense of a fatter paycheck. Too, your reputation for reliability is somewhat weakened each time you say no, especially if you are saying it too often. Reassess your priorities if you possibly can. You may begin to work much more regularly.

And finally, if none of the above applies, you'd better take a closer look at your performance.

AM I EARNING ENOUGH?

This is somewhat related to whether you are working enough, of course. Since you know the daily pay rate in your area, it follows that if you work as many days as you need to, the result will be reflected in your check.

Again, investigate the possibility of registering in other nearby school districts. Consider making yourself available for a greater number of grade levels and classes. Make it a point to accept more assignments.

There is another aspect to this issue, however, and it varies from state to state and between districts. What is required in your area to make you eligible for long-term assignments? For special classes at higher per diem pay rates? If a college course or two can qualify you for more regular work or higher pay rates, what are you waiting for?

Check first in your own district to determine if and how you may increase your earning power while staying close to home. Then remember that inner city districts often pay more than the outlying ones.

A year ago, you might not have been willing to make the drive. Perhaps you doubted your ability to handle these oftimes more difficult groups of students. By now you have many months of subbing experience under your belt. You may find the challenge rewarding. If the thirty-mile drive to the city means the difference between $40 per day and $60, accepting the challenge can increase your paycheck significantly.

AM I REQUESTED BY TEACHERS AND PRINCIPALS?

Being requested as a sub is unquestionably an ego booster. It means that you're doing a darn good job; that others have confidence in your ability. It may also mean, since many districts fill requests first, that you are working more regularly and earning more money than a slapdash colleague!

In a sense, requests to sub are the only means available to school districts for recognizing a job well done. If you're not getting a fair share of requests, what are the reasons behind it?

Is it district policy? Some districts prefer to use a strict rotation system. If this is true in your area, it is a factor beyond your control. Find recognition of your good work in the smiles of the kids when they see you coming and the acceptance of the staff when you check in.

If it isn't district policy, then something in your performance needs sprucing up. Do you take adequate care of room and property? If a teacher returns to find two reams of art paper gone and a fleet ofmangled paper airplanes in a trashcan battlefield, the chances are slim you'll be asked to return. This sort of evidence points not only to your lack of respect for materials but to a probable lack of control on your part as well. Be sure that you distribute materials with discretion and allow for a period of adequate cleanup time before the children are dismissed.

Do you leave the teacher's classroom materials in order? Do you correct whatever tests you possibly can? Do you leave good notes about what's been done today? Say thanks for good ideas or lesson plans? All of these little courtesies—as well as the reactions of the students—can be cause for continued invitations to sub.

Finally, are you putting enough of yourself into your work? Enough ideas in your special bag of tricks? Plodding dully through the day won't make an impression on anyone. Maintaining order and following the lesson plan may in themselves be grounds for being asked to return. Adding your own unique brand of interest and variety can make you a stand-out sub.

Make the most of your talents and your timefillers. Enjoy yourself. Take an interest in the kids you have today. Good news travels fast. When the word gets out that you are not only responsible but versatile as well, your success and your requests will be insured.

Take the time to analyze your performance in light of the questions discussed here. Make a list of your strong points and your weak points. In what areas can you effect a change?

Nowhere is it written in stone that we must love our jobs. Many people work because they have to. But making the most of the job we do can make us feel better all around. If you feel good about the job you've done, then give yourself a pat on the back. You've earned it.

As you begin your second year and your third, your confidence and reputation grow. Problems that once loomed larger than life are handled with the ease of your experience.

A second grader told me not long ago, "Reading is easier than anything!" "I'll bet you didn't always think that," I said. "When did you decide it was easy?"

He frowned into space with Plato-like contemplation, his lower lip pursed into a knot. "I guess," he said finally, with the nod of the sage, "I guess—when I knew I could do it!"

19.

Ideas for Growth and Sharing

In the event you haven't grasped the idea so far, I like sub-bing. I heartily recommend it as a wonderful choice for anyone qualified and interested in kids. In my view, it offers a diversity of experience and a flexibility of time commitment unequaled by any other part-time work. But it isn't perfect. It has its drawbacks. One of the biggest is—loneliness.

Loneliness? You newcomers may be surprised. How on earth is it possible to be lonely surrounded by kids and staff? Because, dear friends, as a noted philosopher once said, it is possible to be in this world but not of it. For a sub it is not only possible, it is inherent in the job to be in the school setting but not of it.

A sub is a stranger, an interloper of sorts—well liked and appreciated perhaps, but nevertheless a temporary presence who comes and goes with the tides of necessity but in truth does not belong anywhere.

Who are his peers? With whom does he share the pride and the problems peculiar to his line of work? With other subs, of course. But where are these other subs? Temporarily present all over the district, but out of his reach and camaraderie.

This is the single greatest complaint I have heard from substitute teachers nationwide, this absence of a peer group of one's own. Apart from a brief, introductory meeting hosted by some districts at the beginning of each school year, there is no further contact between district subs—no meetings, no seminars, no sharing of ideas and/or difficulties.

Is it any wonder, then, given the prevailing attitude of sink or swim, that so many subs who enter the field in September with vast enthusiasm and firm commitment are gone by the first signs of frost? Is it surprising that the need for new subs continues to grow while the available number of full-time positions declines?

Considering the dearth of training common in most areas, the wonder is not that so many subs drop out but that any of us succeed. The school of hard knocks is a time-honored training ground, but surely there's an easier way.

It is my fond hope, of course, that this book will ease the way by helping you to know what to expect and preparing you to handle it. But I'm going to go a step further here and propose what many of you have suggested is missing from the subbing scene: a community of subs.

SUBS CLUBS

Lest the unionizers and the organizers descend, I am not recommending complex associations. I am advocating simple district-wide subs clubs, informal get-togethers whose purpose is the sharing of ideas.

Interested subs, contacted through the district's roster, might choose to attend such informal meetings where contact with other subs is the primary function and learning the common goal. Teachers have seminars and staff meetings.

Why not something similar for subs?

How do you handle class arguments? Troublemakers? Where can I find new ideas? What about the child who refuses to participate? What is it like in the high schools? This is the place to bring up the questions that you never knew whom to ask.

"I had a kid who. . . ." "The other day. . . ." Funny little anecdotes that elicit glassy-eyed stares around the dinner table can find acceptance and commiseration here. Who but the people who share your problems can appreciate your common concerns?

If such a sharing group does not exist in your area and if you find the idea appealing, start one! Meet once each month or twice a year—as rarely or as frequently as you like. But give yourselves the benefit of each other's experience for the growth and improvement of the whole.

RESOURCE CENTERS

Resource centers are an excellent source for the birth of new ideas. Every school district has one full of audiovisual materials, teaching kits, and more for use by teachers at all grade levels. Rarely do subs find their way to these storehouses simply because they don't know they exist. Yet information of all kinds is there for the asking, if you care to track it down.

Occasionally, many resource centers offer hands-on workshops teaching craft ideas, dramatics, and classroom practices. Subs are usually not excluded from attending but neither are they specifically invited. Check with your district office for the location of the resource center and a list of any upcoming workshops.

There's a bit of a double bind here about the entire subbing situation. Some teachers and administrators feel that subs don't put forth enough effort. Subs, on the other hand, feel they'd make the effort if they had any idea where to turn.

Resource centers and teacher workshops are an ideal place to begin. They can offer ideas, education, and support in a constructive atmosphere with lots of peer contact and communication.

PERIODICALS

Too, there are magazines—excellent journals published for teachers each month. They are full of ideas for projects and activities that you can apply to your classes. Because many are offered solely on a subscription basis, they are not readily accessible to subs.

Check with the library for sample copies or ask a teacher you know. Select your favorite and subscribe to it. You'll never run out of ideas.

And speaking of magazines, don't forget those published for children. Geared for various age groups, they offer stories, puzzles, and craft ideas that you can use over and over. The stories are short and often seasonal, making them good choices for the sub. Games and activity pages are usually designed for quick completion, another boon for the sub who plans to use them to occupy the early birds or fill in an odd few moments.

Going stale is an occupational hazard for substitutes. Separated from others who are doing the same job, popping in and out of new classes daily, rarely getting feedback from the teachers for whom you've pinch-hit, you may find it tough to maintain your spark. Who appreciates what you're doing, anyway, you wonder. Who cares what a super sub you are?

The tendency for many, as the year progresses, is to let standards slide. Taking the easy way out is certainly a human frailty. Of course creativity drains your energy. Of course it's easier to pass out paper and say, "Draw what you like," than to initiate a paper sculpture project. And if the class is reasonably quiet, why not let it go at that?

Some subs do. So do some teachers. The losers are the children they teach. The kids learn the lessons and they keep the peace, but they are inspired to nothing more. It's the teacher who gives that little something extra—and expects as much from students—who gives the child a model for success.

Granted, as a sub, your influence is temporary. No miracles are going to take place. But a whiff of inspiration to become, to try, to do, can be a very heady tonic to a child. Why settle for boredom and apathy when you can raise a little interest instead? A drawing taken home to Mom may be just another drawing. But a paper sculpture says, "Look what *I* did!"

A sub in Illinois writes, "I get so tired of walking into a class in the morning and hearing, before I've even begun, 'Oh, yuck! A sub!'"

Maybe, if we all give it our best shot, Illinois, we can turn the frowns to smiles of anticipation.

Don't let the absence of feedback slow you down. The fact that you continue to work is proof you're doing the job. It's nice to hear a teacher say, "Thanks. My class really enjoyed you." But the super sub is too busy subbing to wait for the sound of applause.

LONG-TERM SUBBING

An alternative to full-time teaching that offers some of the benefits of both worlds is long-term subbing. Again depending upon the criteria set by your state or school district, you may be able to teach in the same classroom for thirty days to several months with proper certification. Such opportunities arise when the regular teacher is going to be away from the classroom for an extended period of time, as in the case of maternity leave, personal illness, and so on.

As a long-term sub you may enjoy higher pay, increased subsidiary benefits, and continuity in the classroom. You may still have some time off between assignments for your personal or professional commitments.

Check the chart in Chapter 2 to review the standards for long-term subbing required in your area. Doublecheck your qualifications with the school districts in which you wish to work. If all systems are "go," terrific!

Whichever route you decide to take—the long-term options or the flexibility of day-to-day subbing—be receptive to new ideas. Ideas and encouragement are the substitute's stock in trade. They are the lifeblood of your enthusiasm, and enthusiasm is the best tool you have.

Contrary to the rumblings of the "survival school" of subbing, you are neither a babysitter nor a second-class citizen in the hierarchy of education. The service you perform is a necessary one. Without you, a lot of classrooms would be empty. Furthermore, you have the means and the option to make that service meaningful and vital.

Find ideas by reading and sharing. Seek encouragement and growth from the variety of resources we've explored. Above all, take pride in the job you do, and do it the best way you can.

ABOUT FULL-TIME TEACHING

Some subs, after working regularly for months or years, begin to long for a little continuity. Tired of so many anonymous faces flashing past at roll calls like bolts over the assembly line, they begin to wonder what it might be like to be able to plan for tomorrow. The same thirty shining faces peering up at them expectantly every morning holds a certain keen appeal.

Day-to-day subs whose paychecks reflect only the per diem compensation for their efforts muse about how much larger those checks would be if they were teaching full time. They know it is not unusual for new full-time positions to be filled from the ranks of qualified subs who are willing to assume the responsibilities.

The key word here is qualified. Bearing in mind that each state maintains its own criteria for teacher certification, look into the conditions for qualification wherever you live if the lure of full-time teaching enchants you. A taste of the subbing life has led many a part-timer back to the halls of academe in pursuit of a credential. There is no reason why you cannot be among them.

Consider that along with a class of one's own, the new teacher gets a bigger paycheck, subsidiary benefits like insurance and pension plans—and a lot of new headaches. Your once part-time career is now a full-time commitment. The responsibility for lesson planning and long-range goals is yours. The children's ongoing problems and parental involvement (or the lack of it) are part of your new milieu, not to mention grading, staff meetings, and a raft of other new chores. Before you decide that the grass is greener, be sure the trade-off is worth it to you.

Most important of all, consider that full-time positions are not always easy to find these days. School enrollment is shrinking everywhere. Although substitutes are always in demand, be sure that the likelihood of full-time employment exists in your area before you make the effort to secure it.

If you already have a valid teaching credential, a stint of subbing may be the easiest and surest way to obtain the full-time position you want. Successful subs are noticed. If you are newly certified or new in the area and teaching positions are scarce, make your entrance as a sub. The school district will welcome you with open arms and, if you're good, will happily consider you for full-time employment as soon as the opportunity arises.

20.

On Subbing

A potpourri of inklings and insights, musings and memo-rabilia on the high art of substitute teaching . . . from the people who know it best!

As I neared the completion of this book an intriguing fancy struck me. Wouldn't it be fun, I thought, to include ideas and anecdotes from subs all over the country? The collec-tive voice of far-flung experience has a host of stories to tell.

Come to think of it, why not include the observations and insights of the kids whom these substitutes teach? And teachers! How do they feel about subs? What advice, what insights could they share?

Thanks to a veritable avalanche of responses from my invitations in *Instructor* magazine and in Dick Lochte's col-umn in *The Los Angeles Times,* here they are: candid com-ments "On Subbing" from the people who know it so well. File them away in your memory bank, and may they add to your success.

FROM THE KIDS

There are two kinds of substitutes, judging from the notes I received from kids: those who are "mean" and those who are "nice."

"Mean" subs don't smile. They glare at you through "beady little black eyes" (a commonly-noted physical characteristic) and "jump down your throat for every little thing." They punish the entire class for the transgressions of a few and they never, repeat, never "do anything fun."

"Nice" subs, on the other hand, are recognized by their smiles and their warmth. "They know lots of games and fun stuff to do" and are "happy to help you with your work."

The perfect sub, according to the nearest composite I could draw from their letters, is "nice and fun, strict but not too strict, and knows what we are studying about." It helps if you are reasonably attractive.

The kids seem equally divided in their reactions to finding a substitute in their classrooms. About half become "tense," "upset," or just plain "miserable," fearing that it will be an awful day. The other half are almost overjoyed. "Maybe we won't have to work as much," they hope. Or, "At least I don't have to stare at my same old teacher today."

Once the sub is installed in the classroom, the kids make a lot of snap judgments. "I can tell if a sub is good," says one confident sixth grader, "as soon as she opens her mouth. If she's bored to death and never cracks a smile, she's going to be bad. If she sounds like she's having a good time, we'll have a good time, too."

"Bad subs are never relaxed," notes a fourth grader. "They start out all nervous and frustrated-looking and I say to myself, 'Uh oh!'"

"I look out for the subs who start out by saying, 'I've been a teacher for twenty years.' Usually, you can tell that they haven't because they're the ones who never know what's going on."

"I get a twitchy feeling," says a fifth grader, "if a sub doesn't look kind of everyday normal, like they could be somebody's Mom or Dad. Sometimes I get fooled, but usually the weird ones stay weird."

Talk about getting fooled! A sixth grader writes, "The last sub we had made me skeptical and scared. First of all, he carried a guitar! What kind of sub takes a guitar to school? But he turned out to be great. He knew how to do all the work and then we sang Beatles songs till time to go home and everyone in school was jealous."

Having made these snap judgments, kids say that certain kinds of behavior on the part of the sub can tip the balance one way or the other.

"I once had a sub I called Mrs. Geyser. Every time you said a word, she blew her top!"

"I hate subs who give assignments and then stare at us while we work. They never get involved. They don't want to help. They act like they don't even want to be there."

"Subs who have fun things to do between assignments are the best. They don't just make us sit there and read silently to ourselves all day."

"I once had a sub who looked awful, but she was great. I don't know how she did it, but she actually made math fun."

"I don't like subs who don't spell my name right or say it wrong without asking. It makes everyone laugh."

"Once a sub was mad at the class and I used to stutter. I asked her a question and she answered by stuttering on purpose. A sub should never make fun of you."

A good sense of humor and a well-filled bag of tricks are high-priority qualities in a sub. So is knowing how to do the work. "If a sub doesn't know how to do the work he gives us, it makes me mad. How am I supposed to learn it if he can't teach it?"

No child was able to tell me why kids expect more in the way of entertainment from a sub than they do from their regular teachers. Perhaps because, when the cat's away, the little mice like to play. In any case, "fun stuff" is high on their lists and the sub who provides it will have an easier time with her students.

And knowing how to control a class is extremely important—even when the class is out to trap you:

"A lot of kids try to take advantage of a sub, like giving wrong information. Fortunately, other kids tell the truth but sometimes the sub gets confused."

"A sub has to see what's going on," observes one exasperated child. "Sometimes notes and pictures are being passed right under their nose and they don't even see it!"

And what about when they do see it?

"A sub has to be 'disciplint,'" as one fourth grader put it. "They shouldn't let the class get crazy."

"You shouldn't let us get away with things," urges another. "You should make us think you know what's going on!"

"You have to be strict with the first few kids who do bad things," advises one youngster. "Or else the whole class will try to get away with it."

On the other hand, the kids point out, you should always make the punishment fit the crime.

"Don't take it out on the whole class," says one, "just because a few kids are bad."

"It's not fair to take away everybody's recess because two or three kids are acting stupid."

"Do whatever you say you're going to do. But don't flip out over nothing."

I recently asked a gifted sixth grade class to write essays on what makes a good sub. From Keith Johnson's wonderful youngsters, I'd like to share this one with you:

"First, a good sub should have a fairly good sense of humor. Second, he or she should not let too many people

214   **Where Do I Go from Here?**

get away with things and should not be too austere, just strict enough to let students know he or she means business. In the good sub I also seek friendliness and the quality of being funny with some good projects to do. Finally, any sub needs to know the work pretty well and have some idea what the class is doing."

Bravo. Who says our kids aren't being educated?

FROM THE TEACHERS

Judging by the sparse representation in my mailbox, teachers are reluctant to talk about subs, at least for public consumption. Much of the mail I did get was from teachers who've done some subbing themselves and could see from both sides of the fence.

Gail Davies of Chicago speaks for many of them. "I've been a sub and I know how tough it can be to deal with the spur of the moment. I usually leave a lesson plan with some gaps in it and suggest that the sub either 'do her own thing' or fill in with dittoed puzzles and games, which I leave on the desk just in case."

Ann B. of Austin, Texas, is always hopeful that the sub will contribute something original. "Sometimes I get back and the kids will show me some super art project or something and I know from their excitement the sub was good."

"What I dread," writes Bonnie Mueller from Ohio, "is coming back to school and the first thing the kids ask is, 'What did the substitute say about us?' Too often that means they gave him or her a rough time and now they don't want me to know."

"We usually hear about it from the other teachers," writes Kaye S. from Philadelphia, "if our kids were wild in the playground or something and the sub didn't seem to have much control. We prize the subs who can keep control and ask for them whenever we can."

But that's difficult, according to a Covina, California, teacher. "We can ask for the subs we know are good, but we can't always get them. Maybe they're already booked elsewhere. We always have to assume it may be someone new and leave plenty of stuff to keep them busy."

"I appreciate a sub who keeps my things in order and follows the instructions I leave," writes an Omaha teacher. "It's nice when they get the papers corrected, too. It's easier for me when I get back."

One Glendora, California, teacher leaves answer codes for tests and worksheets. "That way, I know the papers will be corrected properly and I won't have to review them."

Nancy McMullen of Covina once came back after a lengthy absence to find six weeks' worth of uncorrected papers. "You can be sure I never asked for him again."

On the other hand, a sixth grade teacher from Trenton, New Jersey, says, "I have had subs who worked all the problems, made up an answer sheet, and had the kids correct the papers themselves. That's the kind of efficiency and foresight I appreciate when I'm out unexpectedly."

A Wisconsin teacher who was unexpectedly out for five days recently had no time to leave an adequate lesson plan. "I left some hurried suggestions with the principal and left town on an emergency. I have to say the sub I had was marvelous. She was very enthusiastic and had a lot of good ideas of her own, but she covered a lot of academic ground, too. I telephoned long distance once because I was worried about what was going on. But this woman had everything under control. I wish there were more like her."

Many teachers tell me they prepare for a sub by writing out lesson assignments and telling the class in advance, if they can, that they expect business as usual.

Georgia Florentine, a former teacher, now principal of Ben Lomond School in Covina, says she tried very hard not to get sick because of the time and effort it took just to get ready for a sub. "I wanted the sub to come in and enjoy my class without having to worry too much about keeping them busy.

"Some subs have lots of initiative and good ideas and that's wonderful if you're lucky enough to get one. But many seem to want to rely on whatever the teacher has left. Since you don't always know which kind you'll get, you have to be well prepared."

Ideally, the sub will have creativity and self-reliance but will follow the patterns a teacher has established in the classroom. "One sub," says teacher Evelyn Kemble, "tried to undermine everything I had set up. She told the kids repeatedly that her way was the best way and that they should report to me what I was doing wrong!"

If kids see good subs as strict but fun and wise in the ways of the classroom, teachers see them much the same way. What seems to come through underlined in red is: Keep control, have all the fun you want on your own, but don't veer too far from what's expected.

Good advice.

FROM THE SUBS

If there is a common denominator among the many subs whose anecdotes, nostalgia, and timely tips poured in, it is surely their unfailing good humor. They seem to share a gift for seeing the bright side of things and for appreciating the fresh outlook and inherent charm of children.

Corinne Craighead of Salem, Oregon, whose letter arrived in a gaily hand-decorated envelope that bespeaks her own originality, contributes these delightful one-liners which she has heard from primary students in her first year of subbing: "My Dad and him were born the same age but they're not the same old." "The volcano was supposed to interrupt." "I got invited to her house tomorrow cuz it's her lucky day." "Look! The raindrops are leaking!" And this classic: "I forgot to tell you, Miss Craighead. I have poison oak!"

Children are very literal creatures, Corinne points out. "Once I asked the class to clean off their desks. Instead of merely removing their work, they rose in a body and proceeded with wet towels and soap!"

Nearly identical slips of the juvenile tongue were reported by substitutes Cheryl Boyd of Lubbock, Texas, and Mary Sholty of Los Angeles. Each tells of students (distantly related?) who asked shyly, "Are you our prostitute today?"

And Dolly Knee of Santa Ana, California, makes a game of her unusual last name. "There's a rhyme I've made up to introduce myself to primary students," she says. "It ends with 'I'm not Mrs. Ear and I'm not Mrs. Eye . . . Tell me, tell me, who am I?' While most youngsters guess 'Mrs. Foot or Mrs. Hand,'" Dolly laughs, "I will never forget the child who piped up, 'Mrs. Booby?'"

Iowa Honn of Oxford, Iowa, who has been subbing for twenty-five years, is aware of the tendency children have to call 'em as they see 'em. "We were discussing deer one day," she says, "and a child asked if I knew how to tell a deer from a buck. Before I could answer, a little boy yelled, 'I know! A buck has two big . . .'

"Afraid of what was coming, I interrupted quickly. But the child grinned and said, 'It's okay. I was only going to say two big antlers!'"

Mrs. Honn's embarrassment leaps off the page. "Guess whose face was red?"

But sometimes the little faux pas slip out when you least expect them. Mrs. Honn taught kindergarten one day when a little fellow had trouble with his fly. Each time he went to the restroom adjoining the classroom, she had to help him zip up.

The next day when he went to the restroom, he was gone a long time. Stopping at the door, she asked solicitously, "Richie? Do you need some help?"

The youngster answered proudly, "No, thanks, Mrs. Honn. I oiled the little (bleep) last night!"

Without a doubt, children are outspoken. Jeff Staddler of Manitowoc, Wisconsin, is often asked, "Are you a giant?"

And Jeanne C. from New York, who struggled to lose forty pounds one summer, was eyed warily by a first grader in September. After a moment, the child asked accusingly, "Aren't you the one who was fat?"

My own friend, Bobbi Maass, who subs in Azusa and is far from fat was stung to the quick with, "Are you pregnant?"

Then there are the mishaps. Iowa Honn walked into a science class one 90-degree day and found the plastic fish-tanks collapsed from the heat. "Begging buckets and scoops from the custodian," she recalls, "the kids and I went fishing!"

Debbie Collier of Candor, New York, discovered after one day of lunchroom duty that kids and squirt bottles don't mix. "The next day, I raced to get to the cafeteria first so I could gather up all the ketchup and mustard. The kids had to come to me to be served and it must have been quite a sight to see a substitute in the lunchroom hoarding twenty squirt bottles in front of me," she writes. But disaster was averted and that's what counts.

Sometimes disaster is not averted. Corinne Craighead discovered three snakes in a jar in a little girl's desk—after the jar was broken!

And when the hutch door came loose in a first grade room one day, Jean Tyler and her little San Diego charges spent the day mopping up "rabbit doo"!

A lot has changed about subbing over the years. Catherine Briggs of Laguna, California, was subbing in Los Angeles fifty years ago. "In those days we all trooped downtown to a central office in the mornings and sat there to see if we'd be called. My subjects were English and History but I was given Math and Chemistry classes, and once, even Metal Welding!

"Rarely was there a lesson plan. We were strictly on our own and always in a different place. Eventually, papers were prepared for subs telling them at least where things were located. Before that, you counted yourself lucky if you could find the restroom between classes.

"The worst part about it," Miss Briggs recalls, "is that subs were treated like nonpeople. Regular teachers talked around you but never to you in the staff room and if cake was passed, it wasn't to us. Once, the head of the Language Department escorted me to lunch. It was a kindness I've never forgotten."

The cattle-call approach has disappeared, of course, with the demise of the central office. Lesson plans are commonplace and most subs are treated with courtesy if not with outright friendship by the staff.

Yet Mary Sholty of Los Angeles, subbing in the same school district some fifty years later, still feels unappreciated much of the time. "I love the freedom of free-lance teaching," she says. "I've been doing it for years and I really enjoy the kids and the job. But I sure remember it when I hear a 'thank you' from the staff. It simply doesn't happen often enough."

Paul Vendeland of Los Angeles also feels subs are "at the low end of the totem pole." Still, he enjoys the freedom subbing gives him and thinks it's "getting better all the time."

Paul's favorite story involves an elementary school principal for whom Paul has worked a lot. The man was known for his fairness to students. No exceptions or concessions were made with regard to discipline or circumstances. "One day," Paul chuckles, "we were in the lunch line together when he asked for a double serving of vegetables instead of potatoes. The server, a student who knew him well, smiled jauntily. 'Sorry, sir—we can't make any exceptions!'"

Catherine Briggs recalls that she got her first subbing assignment as a result of a flu epidemic fifty years ago. Iris Haines of West Covina still complains, "I feel like an ambulance chaser! I love the challenge and the freedom and all, but I never get to work unless someone's sick."

Some subs are still bothered over the loss of their own identities. "When I was asked, 'Who are you?' at a school, I replied, 'Elsa Poole,'" writes a lady from Athens, Ohio. "But the questioner looked at me blankly. Finally, she asked rather frostily, 'I mean, for whom are you subbing?'"

Others take the change of hats in stride. "I realize," writes Ann Fahey of Washington, "that the teacher means no disrespect by asking me, 'Who are you today?' It's simple curiosity and sometimes a conversation-opener. I just smile and tell him *both* my names."

Subs have had their share of embarrassing moments. For Deborah Collier, it was pulling an assignment in a music class to find it was instrumental and not voice. "I can manage 'Happy Birthday,'" she writes. "But I can't play any instrument except the kazoo. I went into shock when I had to give a tuba lesson, of all things. I listened with interest as the student played his piece. And I managed, 'Well, it sounds okay to me!'"

For Minta Theriot, a registered nurse in Devers, Texas, who decided to try some subbing, it was finding herself in a junior high math class that was working on a factor tree. "The students were confused as to how to proceed and I hated to admit that factoring was beyond me. So I called on a supersharp boy and asked him to demonstrate the process. He jumped at the chance to show off his skills and soon had numbers and lines branching out into factors all over the blackboard.

"When some students complained that they couldn't understand, I asked Mark to explain what he was doing. Whereupon he gave me a woeful look and said, 'I guess I only know how to *do* it, but not much about how to *tell* it.'

"By that time, thankfully, I had recognized the logic in the maze of numbers and I think I looked pretty smart to those kids as I explained the process to them!"

In a sense, this is how we all proceed, testing the unfamiliar waters until we feel comfortable; using whatever tips and tricks and unforeseen support come our way.

Ann Christy of Parma, Ohio, was new in town when she began subbing. "I had taught first and second grade in another state," she explains, "but I was scared to death of the upper grades." Unfortunately, my first subbing call was for a sixth grade and, not wanting to hurt my future chances, I accepted.

"The teacher was well prepared, but I assumed the class would be uncontrollable and I would fall apart. Much to my surprise, everything went smoothly and I really enjoyed the class. But I was still not convinced that I could handle it until one boy said, as he was leaving, 'Please come back again. You were great!' I've never forgotten those kind words. They've made it easier for me many times since."

A young man from New Hampshire writes in a similar vein. "When I started subbing I was afraid the little kids might have difficulty relating to me, a man, since most of their regular teachers are women. But most of them find it's kind of fun to have a man teacher. They ask for me when they know their teacher is going to be out. I'm not sure whether it's me or the novelty."

Many of us finally come to rely on our experience and intuitions. Dozens of subs suggested, "Carry a good book for reading aloud, no matter what else you may use."

Carol Verhoef of Glendora, California, carries a "goodie bag" of short puzzles and activities as well. Each goodie can be completed quickly by anyone who has finished the work "so the child feels he has accomplished something."

Carol finds it helpful to wear clothing with pockets so that keys and whistles are at hand. And no matter what grade she teaches (K–6) she has each child introduce himself in the morning. "It takes a little extra time," she writes, "but it's worth it. Each child has at least one opportunity to speak with me personally. I learn a little about him and I love to watch the facial expressions."

Sometimes we call on our own inner strengths—those talents and perceptions we spoke of. Minta Theriot, the R.N. from Texas, was delighted to be assigned to a health class. "I was called upon to teach about intestinal parasites and I drew on my nursing background to cover it fully. I thought I had handled it pretty well, but that night I got a call from a friend whose daughter had been in my class.

"My friend said, 'Kim came home complaining about your teaching.' I was so disappointed. Then she added, 'She'll never forget your lesson. It seems your descriptions were so graphic, they made her sick to her stomach!'"

A sub needs ingenuity. I fell over laughing at this letter, sent by Nancy Small of Sturgeon Bay, Wisconsin. It is a classic in perception and quick thinking:

A friend of mine was nervously subbing in the ninth grade for the first time. As the students filed in, it was easy to identify the "ringleader." The clever sub overheard the ringleader's name and just as the class quieted down for the roll call, she smiled at him and said, "Hi, Larry! Be sure and tell your Mom hi for me!"

Larry remained docile the entire class period, apparently trying to figure out how—or if—the sub really knew his mother!

*   *   *

For sheer resourcefulness, patience, and for. stitute teachers take the prize. They face Pandor. every morning and handle it with humor, tact, and—y. affection.

Catherine Briggs noted that fifty years ago "the plus side of subbing was that one's ingenuity was tested and one either made it or one didn't." Some things, it seems, never change.

Today, Iowa Honn, still subbing at the age of seventy-two, chuckles with amusement at the years and the problems. "This is the life," she says. "It surely keeps me young!"

Epilogue

In the preceding chapters I have tried to give the reader a fair and objective look at substitute teaching today. It's not the easiest job in the world nor, indeed, the highest paid. Yet it offers a unique opportunity for many of you, who perhaps never knew you were qualified, to embark on a rewarding, challenging, and flexible career in part-time teaching.

Certainly the letters I have shared with you from subs all over the country reflect far more in the way of satisfaction and optimism than in disappointment or gloom. They seem to emphasize that good subbing can be downright fun. Letters from cheerful and successful substitute teachers who face hordes of average, reasonably bright, and happy youngsters daily came to me by the hundreds.

But there were other letters, too. There were only a handful and perhaps, with a reasonably clear conscience, I could choose to ignore them. Still, they nag at my attention because they reflect a totally different kind of subbing experience. It is to these few letter writers and all of you who may have shared similar experiences that I feel compelled to speak now.

These letter writers, without exception from inner-city and ghettolike areas all over the country, share a common disillusionment with the educational system in general and with substitute teaching in particular. Faced with apathy or outright violence in the classroom, helpless to cope with the wall of disrespect and value rejection that blocks the way toward learning, these people have given up all hope of even the smallest measure of success.

It is difficult for even the regular faculty, these subbing dropouts say, to maintain any semblance of order in a setting where survival is the highest ambition and failure is a way of life. "I have seen knifings, beatings, and attempted rape in the corridors," says one former sub. "I still have nightmares wondering if I could have prevented them. How can I hope to communicate with these kids when I am in constant fear for my own safety?"

It is a sad reflection on our time and society that such horror exists in some schools. Yet snug in the bosom of placid suburbia, I am aware that it does exist. And while it is rare—while most of you will never deal with it—it is a problem we cannot ignore.

Someone must stand at the head of these classrooms. In the temporary absence of the more experienced regular teacher, some sub must deal with these kids. If this is the kind of area in which you will sub, you need to be amply prepared.

The four keys to good subbing are more than ever necessary here. Your positive attitude can be your greatest ally, and honesty the means to your success.

Meet these students on their own ground. Since the likelihood of imparting new values on such a temporary basis is nil, deal with their values head on. Make it clear that, since you must live with each other for a day or two, you intend that all of you make the best of it.

Set up a reward system for positive behavior that corresponds with the policies of the school and use it for all it is worth. Emphasize timefillers, assignments, and activities that students can handle with relative ease so that the ratio of success is high.

As a substitute from Detroit, Michigan, points out, "The only way to deal with these kids is to try to make them feel good about themselves. If I can somehow get them to believe that I like and respect them, I usually get the same in return."

Above all, be alert to potential troublemakers and potentially dangerous situations. Don't attempt to be a martyr or a hero. Ask for help when conditions warrant it and do not be hesitant to ask that certain students be removed from your classroom. Better to share the responsibility for authority than to carry it alone and make mistakes.

If you can follow the prescribed principles for procedure and discipline, if you can make full use of the resourcefulness and flexibility I have stressed as vital assets, and if you can maintain a sense of humor and patience when frustration ravels your sleeve—then perhaps you will find, rising above the discontent, acceptance and some degree of accomplishment.

The hope is that somehow tomorrow's perspectives may ease the problems of the ghetto school. For now, we must deal with present realities no matter where we live.

In Podunk or Metropolis, kids are kids and problems of all kinds arise. Schools will continue to open their doors and to overcome these problems as best they can. And for all of its problems, the system still works. To one extent or another, most kids do learn to read and write, and sometimes—thank heavens—to think.

For the teacher it's a monumental and rewarding accomplishment. For the sub, it's no less a source of pride.

Good luck and good subbing!

APPENDIX A

SOURCES FOR MORE BRIGHT IDEAS

Under normal circumstances the bag of tricks provided in Part Three should give you plenty of variety and choice. However, if you wish to expand your repertoire, you might check these sources for indoor and outdoor games, arts and crafts ideas, and creative play activities.

GAMES, PUZZLES, AND TIMEFILLERS

Bannerman, G. and Fakkema, R. *Guide for Recreation Leaders.* Atlanta: John Knox Press, 1975.

Barry, Sheila Anne. *The Super-Colossal Book of Puzzles, Tricks and Games.* New York: Sterling Publishing Co., 1979.

Orlick, Terry. *The Cooperative Sports and Games Book.* New York: Pantheon Books, 1978.

ARTS AND CRAFTS

Alkema, Chester J. *Greeting Cards You Can Make.* New York: Sterling Publishing Co., 1973.

Krinsky, N. and Berry, B. *Paper Construction for Children*. New York: Van Nostrand Reinhold, 1973.

Rockwell, H. *Printmaking*. New York: Doubleday, 1973.

Temko, Simon. *Paper Folding To Begin With*. Indianapolis, IN: Bobbs Merrill, 1968.

CREATIVE PLAY

Howard, Vernon. *Pantomimes, Charades and Skits*. New York: Sterling Publishing Co., 1959.

Howard, Vernon. *The Complete Book of Children's Theater*. New York: Doubleday, 1969.

Shipley, J.T. *Word Play*. New York: Hawthorn Books, 1972.

APPENDIX B

GOOD READING

Most classrooms are equipped with a selection of books from which you may choose for reading aloud. Since your time is limited, however, you may prefer to keep a few of your favorites on hand and stick to short stories whenever possible.

The following recommended reading list includes a few of my favorites as well as suggestions from the Los Angeles County Library, Children's Branch. Many are award-winning new stories, or classics with fanciful illustrations that provide, along with the fun, a wonderful insight into human behavior.

KINDERGARTEN THROUGH THIRD GRADE

Bemelmans, L., *Madeline.* (A series of books.) New York: Viking, 1946.

Conford, E. *Eugene the Brave.* Boston: Little, Brown, 1978.

DeBrunhoff, J. *Babar the Elephant.* New York: Random House, 1966. (A series)

Delton, J. *Three Friends Find Spring*. New York: Crown, 1977.

Harrison, D. *The Book of Giant Stories*. New York: American Heritage, 1972.

Kraus, R. *Leo the Late Bloomer*. New York: Windmill Books, 1971.

Lobel, A. *Fables*. New York: Harper & Row, 1980.

McCloskey, R. *Make Way for Ducklings*. New York: Viking, 1969.

Pearson, S. *Everybody Knows That*. New York: Dial, 1978.

Viorst, J. *Alexander and the Terrible, Horrible, No Good, Very Bad Day*. New York: Atheneum, 1974.

SECOND THROUGH FOURTH GRADE

Anderson, H. C. *The Emperor's New Clothes*. Boston: Houghton Mifflin, 1949.

Calhoun, M. *Goblin Under the Stairs*. New York: Morrow, 1968.

Evans, K. *The Boy Who Cried Wolf*. Chicago: Whitman, 1960.

Godden, R. *The Old Woman Who Lived in a Vinegar Bottle*. New York: Viking, 1972.

Haley, G. *A Story, A Story*. New York: Atheneum, 1970.

Hoke, H. M. *Spooks, Spooks, Spooks*. New York: Franklin Watts, 1966.

Keats, E.J. *The Snowy Day*. New York: Viking, 1972.

McDermott, B. *The Golem*. New York: Lippincott, 1976.

McDermott, G. *Arrow to the Sun*. New York: Viking, 1974.

Mosel, A. *The Funny Little Woman*. New York: Dutton, 1972.

Ness, E. *Do You Have the Time, Lydia?*. New York: Dutton, 1971.

Ransome, A. *The Fool of the World and His Flying Ship*. New York: Farrar, Straus and Giroux, 1968.

Rudolph, M. *The Magic Sack*. New York: McGraw Hill, 1967.

Sleator, W. *The Angry Moon*. Boston: Little, Brown, 1970.

Zemach, H. *Duffy and the Devil*. New York: Farrar, Straus and Giroux, 1973.

FOURTH THROUGH SIXTH GRADE

Farley, C. *Loosen Your Ears.* New York: Atheneum, 1977. (Short
  stories)
Kipling, R. *Just So Stories.* New York: Doubleday, 1952. (Short stories)
Konigsberg, E. *Throwing Shadows.* New York: Atheneum, 1979. (Short
  stories)
Silverstein, S. *Where the Sidewalk Ends* and *The Light in the Attic.* New
  York: Harper & Row, 1974 and 1981. (Poetry)
Sobol, D. *Encyclopedia Brown.* New York: Thomas Nelson, 1975. (A
  series of short mysteries for children to solve)

For older students I like to read classic short stories by
Guy de Maupassant and O. Henry that may be found in
any number of collections. They are wonderful discussion
starters.

I often use *Tales from the Arabian Nights* or *Aesop's Fables,* also widely available, as a lead-in to a whimsical drawing period.

INDEX